VISITS FROM THE FOREST PEOPLE

An Eyewitness Report of Extended Encounters with Bigfoot

Julie Scott
and the Scott Family

foreword by Sali Sheppard-Wolford

Pine Winds Press

Pine Winds Press

An imprint of Idyll Arbor, Inc.

39129 264th Ave SE, Enumclaw, WA 98022

www.PineWindsPress.com

Pine Winds Press Editor: Thomas M. Blaschko

Photographs: Wayne Scott

Cover Painting: Alex Evans

Cover Design: Thomas M. Blaschko

ISBN 9780937663196

*This book is dedicated to our very own "Bigfoot bait,"
our granddaughter Lilee Isabelle whose deeply joyous
laughter and sweet, thoughtful personality attracts
anyone or anything.*

*You are the joy of our lives
We love you.*

Contents

FOREWORD

Julie and I met in early 2010 at the Oregon Sasquatch Symposium after developing a friendship via email and the Oregon Bigfoot forum. When she asked me to write something to be included in her upcoming book, *Visits from the Forest People*, I found myself in a quandary. Although I am a spiritual person, I do not adhere to any religious belief system, and I wondered how I could write something without offending anyone (including Julie) in the process.

Then I read the book and discovered it doesn't matter. *Visits from the Forest People* speaks to all of us. The fact that it includes experiences some might find paranormal or supernatural (evil) should not matter either. The word supernormal (beyond what is thought to be normal or natural) better describes some of the things both Julie's family and my family have experienced. The fact that four credible adults write in their own words of similar experiences in *Visits from the Forest People* lends credence to their claims. The fact that many of their experiences mirrored those of my own family and friends reinforces what I have heard from numerous long-term witnesses. To me, the fact that science cannot/will not accept, or even bother to look into this type of experience, is irrelevant. Some things cannot be proved.

Those with an open mind will find much to ponder in *Visits from the Forest People*. We have only scratched the surface in our knowledge of Sasquatch. There ARE no experts in this field. The closest thing to experts we have are the folks who have had daily interactions with these elusive giants on a long-term basis.

If you really listen to what is being said in *Visits from the Forest People*, you will find yourself reassessing everything you thought you knew about Sasquatch. They are NOT some big, dumb ape that lives in the woods. They are people; like us, but not like us. They are extremely intelligent and completely in tune with the world they live in. We are not. Their main concern is survival, but they are curious about the puny, hairless ones who share their planet.

I thank Julie, and her family for having the courage to write this book.

Sali Sheppard-Wolford

August 2010

PROLOGUE

This is a simple, true, and sometimes frightening account of our family's encounters and experiences with Bigfoot creatures over a six-month period while living off the west coast of Washington State. These events occurred between mid-September 2008 and the end of March 2009.

The events are accurate and real, but we have changed many names to protect and conceal people, locations, and Bigfoot from any harm. Many people believe that Bigfoot is only one creature, since the name looks singular and is usually written with a capital B, suggesting one creature, but in truth there are many "bigfoots," if you will. As you read this account, please keep in mind that the name can be plural, for we absolutely believe we had more than one Bigfoot in our backyard.

Our family consists of my husband Wayne, our two adult daughters in their early 20s, Elizabeth and Rachel, our four-year-old granddaughter Lilee, and me, Julie. Oh, I can't forget our two female Border Collie-mix dogs, Sophie, and Molly.

I am not a writer, none of us are, but we are relating these encounters as simply and accurately as we can. I hope the reality and the depth of the humanity of these forest people is clearly brought out in this narrative, and that readers will understand why, we *strongly* oppose hunting down and killing these beings for any reason.

We are Christians with a traditional Biblical belief in Jesus as Lord and God's Son. We believe in one God, the Creator who loves us deeply and is in control of all that exists. We believe in a supernatural and spiritual world, both good and evil, that influences people, animals, nature, and all living things. We only mention this so you will understand where we are coming from as you read references to our faith throughout this book.

In fact, we would not be surprised if the most opposition to and criticism of our story comes from those in mainstream churches and those who claim to be religious. The reason is that, unfortunately, many believe that anything is from "The Devil" if it's not found in the Bible, cannot be explained, or has paranormal origins, as we believe Bigfoot may have.

Other criticism most likely will come from those who have been in Bigfoot research for many years, but have grown a bit cynical and skeptical because of their lack of scientific "proof" or limited personal experiences involving the cryptid. Although they may claim to be experts, we have found that there are no experts in Bigfoot research. There are only those who investigate possible evidence of Bigfoot creatures.

We deeply appreciate those who have and continue to spend countless hours and dollars from their own pockets in the spirit of true research, not for the sake of pride or money.

For some, this account may not seem to be a scientific addition to Bigfoot research, but we ask you to consider the following: Since no Bigfoot creature has ever been captured alive or found dead as far as is publicly known, what is the reality of these creatures? In fact, Bigfoot data is based mostly on actual sightings by individuals; it is either derived from brief glimpses or from cases of ongoing habitation, as in our case.

People who are involved in ongoing situations are called long-term witnesses. Researchers such as Jane Goodall or Diane Fossey, who studied the chimpanzee and the gorilla, learned about these primates because of their long-term commitment. Many years were spent actually living around them and building a relationship with them.

It is happening in many rural areas across this country, like little ole' grammas feeding the Bigfoot leftovers every day without telling anyone. The knowledge certainly hasn't gotten to the general public. In fact, only a handful of Bigfoot researchers believe in or accept the reality of this. Those involved usually keep quiet because they become protective of the Bigfoot creatures and are afraid of ridicule. The few that have shared their experiences with some research groups have had the whole situation collapse and the relationships destroyed because of "scientific" intrusion: cameras, bait, strangers prowling around at night, and so on. Perhaps it's time for researchers to concentrate more on these long-term relationships instead of just looking for footprints or audio taping vocalizations of a screaming Bigfoot.

More concrete evidence comes from plaster casts of footprints, hair, or blood samples, but they are all inconclusive. Very few videos or pictures exist, so those we do have are constantly being dissected and criticized. What about audio tapes of purported Bigfoot vocalizations, or even more subjective evidence, such as smells, the feeling of being watched, or infrasound reactions? Isn't every bit of information important? We believe so.

So, that is our main intention, to share our experience and contribute to the knowledge of these Bigfoot creatures, small or great as our contribution may be. We also hope our story will encourage others to come forward and tell of their own encounters.

Lastly, we would like to mention that before experiencing what we've written about here, we'd thought there was a possibility of such creatures existing but had never read any books on the subject or researched anything on the internet. Like many people, we saw the famous Patterson/Gimlin footage of a female Bigfoot filmed at Bluff Creek, California or an occasional TV show. Little did we know that all this was about to change.

There's a saying in Bigfoot circles: "You don't find them, they find you."

Oh, how true…

1. In the Beginning

We had searched for many months in several states for a place to live.

The previous winter in eastern Washington had been particularly hard, with five feet of snow on the ground for five straight months. We were all tired of it, so we began to seriously explore the idea of moving to the west coast of Washington or Oregon. We had never lived on the coast before, so it sounded like it might be an exciting adventure. We owned two internet businesses at the time: one was a forest product business and the other marketed medicinal herbs. These gave us a lot of freedom to basically live wherever we wanted.

Little did we know what we were about to encounter.

An opportunity to rent a house on the Washington coast with an option to purchase became available. The home was set in a unique location, surrounded by thick rainforest landscaping.

We had been looking for a place to buy, but we thought it wise to live in an area first to make sure we really liked it before purchasing. We are glad we made that choice. Living on the coast was very different physically, politically, and spiritually. Almost immediately, we realized that we really didn't like the area and its large population. Don't misunderstand, the area was beautiful. The views of Mt. Rainier were stunning, all 14,400 feet of her! The noises of the ocean were new and exciting, yet it still didn't seem to be a match. But we settled in, trusting in the Lord to see what would happen and how things would play out. Besides, we had signed a one-year lease.

Water dripped from the forest canopy all the time, even when it wasn't raining. The smell of the ocean continually filled the air. Salt coated the windshield of the van when it rained. The climate was always damp and cold, chilling you to the bone no matter how many layers of clothing you wore. I quickly took up the habit of drinking many cups of hot tea during the day to help keep warm.

There were other houses not far from ours, but the forest was so dense that except for the occasional bark of a dog, you could not see or hear anything coming from the direction of the other homes. Although we lived next to a main road, there were few sounds or disturbances at our house, only the sounds of many birds, deer, coyote, and other wildlife that frequented our woods.

From our time visiting and living in the mountains and backcountry of the Rockies, we knew that every forest has patterns and rhythms. As you spend time there, you become sensitive and adapted to the ebb and flow of forest life. You expect, or at least learn to expect, certain things to happen. In the Rockies, the leaves of aspens turn a fluttery golden-yellow in the autumn, while the needles of a spruce stay green all year long. Observing for even a short period of time, you might see a vast array of wild animals, from deer and squirrels to bear or even a badger.

Therefore, when we moved into unfamiliar territory to a place where the climate, landscape, and even the people were different, we thought that the familiar lullaby of the forest would help us to adapt. Yet we had barely moved in when bizarre and bewildering events began to transpire. The woods around our new home seemed to have a behavior and character all their own and different from what we were used to.

We quickly became aware of a rather strange and oppressive spiritual atmosphere. I'm sure you have gone somewhere new and had a strange feeling, like "something is not right here," but you can't quite put your finger on the source. We each were having really weird dreams that sometimes woke us up in the middle of the night. What was this place?

There were several locals who obviously loved the area, since they had lived there 15, 20, or even 30 years. We met some nice folks at a local community center during a farmer's market event one Saturday. They welcomed us to "Paradise," in their words.

Anyway, we attributed the strangeness we felt to the previous occupant (and owner) of the house. She was deep into New Age activities and beliefs, including crystal power, pyramid energy, drum beating, and astrology, sprinkled with a hefty dose of a New Age non-traditional Jesus. Wow! In any case, this had created a dark, deceptive, and evil presence, which we prayerfully asked God to change. The atmosphere did begin to change, bringing peace and light instead.

We lived on three acres surrounded by dense rainforest-type foliage consisting mostly of ferns, fir trees, western red cedars, and alders, along with some maple that turned spectacular colors just weeks after we arrived.

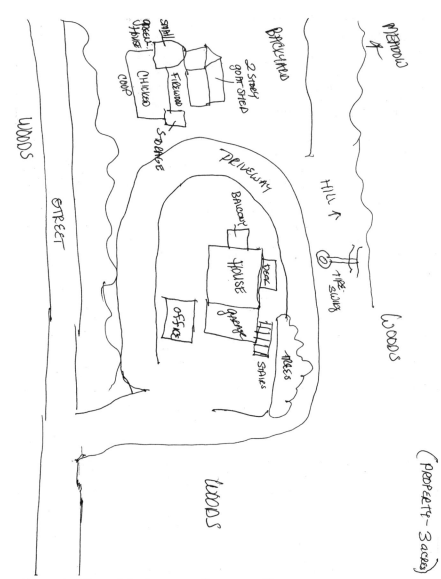

Figure 1: Map of the house and surrounding area.

Figure 2: Driveway on the kitchen side of the house where the hill goes up to the swing area.

Blackberry bushes lined each street and extended their thorny control into the forests. Since no neighbors were visible from the house, the owner had not put curtains on any of the many large windows. The house was large, a tri-level home with a two-car garage tucked under the bedrooms on the top floor. A small, separate building stood only four feet from the front and garage doors on the street side of the house. We used this space for our office.

A small backyard sloped down a small hill out back. It was the only open space and open sky we really had. Not much hope for a spring garden, really. When we climbed the hill near the house, we could see the Olympic Mountains above the tree line. The view of those stunning mountains went on for many, many miles.

Figure 3: The small backyard, with the goat house on the left and the balcony overhead.

Across the driveway, up the hill on the kitchen side of the house, there was an opening in the trees that created a large "room" of sorts. On one of the trees was a tire swing, the rope being hung way up high. It must have required either a very tall ladder or a great plan to tie that rope safely up under the canopy of old-growth Douglas firs. The tire was cut in a way that allowed one's behind to fit snuggly and securely into a deep pocket just for the tush while we could use our hands to hold circular handles on the sides. Elizabeth, Rachel, and Lilee spent many hours swinging, screaming with fear and excitement as they soared back and forth high up in the air. We "older folk" were much more sensible and kept our feet planted on solid ground.

Figure 4: Wooded area where the tire swing hung.

Figure 5: Another shot of the area near the tire swing.

The ground was a thick, spongy carpet made of years of autumn leaf droppings, moss, and twigs. The forest room always had a damp, musty and earthy smell, a fragrance that reminded me of a childhood adventure book from somewhere in the past. It only added to the mystery and made the occupants of the forest seem more mysterious. A surreal place, as surreal as the whole situation was fast becoming.

Within just a few days after moving in, we all began to feel like we were being watched, especially at night, but what was it? This was an eerie, spooky feeling. Could there be men outside cutting boughs and working in the forest behind us? Not at three o'clock in the morning... hopefully. Most people can tell when someone or something is looking at them. At that point I started hanging some curtains, hoping that would help.

Then came the unfamiliar wildlife noises, such as whoops, whistles, howls, owl-like hooting (we also heard real owls hooting, but this was different), clicking and knocking sounds, and strangest of all, a high-pitched teakettle sound — a sort of hand-held-circular-saw-cutting-through-wood type of shriek. In the beginning we had no idea what all of this meant. We heard these sounds during the daytime, as well as at night. Owning a business that supplied other companies with natural products, many of which came from forests, we'd obviously spent many hours for many years out in some deep woods. It is a whole other world out there, but what we were now experiencing was very different... very new... very weird.

Sometimes accompanying the noises, loud, two-footed (bipedal) walking could also be heard. The trees and bushes shook as something or someone heavily walked just out of view from the house. It was totally unlike the gentle sound of deer making their way through the brush.

On the third day after moving in, my husband Wayne heard some of this heavy, loud walking followed by a loud thud, as if something heavy had been picked up and thrown "with a disgruntled attitude" across the brush. Wayne said that whatever creature did the throwing, it didn't sound happy; the object thrown sounded like a hay bale being tossed, although we knew it couldn't be that.

Before this move, we had lived on a 1,200-acre ranch that was surrounded by wilderness. Even before that, we'd lived on 40 acres in the foothills of the Rocky Mountains. We had black bear, grizzlies, cougars, coyotes, bobcats, deer, and all sorts of smaller animals wandering through our yard on a regular basis. We were used to wildlife and their sounds, but this was so very different.

As the four of us began to discuss these incidents, we jokingly spoke of Bigfoot being the reason for all of this strangeness going on. Once we even mentioned something about this to the owner. Her response was that it could be a small monkey that the previous owner before her had released out into the forest behind the house at least ten years earlier. I doubted that critter could still be alive after so many years.

Several weeks later, even after Wayne saw a large, amber-colored eye peering out from behind a bush located just outside of Elizabeth's bedroom window and then briefly caught an outline of a dark, gorilla-like head, we still were not totally sure that it was a Bigfoot. It's a strange thing to try and process it all when you have hardly any knowledge about what is happening.

I need to mention here that there is a strange phenomenon that has occurred with many people who have Bigfoot sightings, although this didn't exactly happen to us. First, the brain says, "What am I really looking at?" Many think it must be a bear, because bears are common and we've all seen a bear, or at least a picture of a bear. When someone sees a Bigfoot, there is usually no past data in their mind related to the present sighting. Therefore, either the brain totally denies the information coming in, or else it deposits the information in a holding tank. Many times, the information is retrieved days, months, or even years later, when the original sighting is vividly relived with the feelings, smells, etc. associated with the sighting. It's the same type of post-traumatic symptom that some people experience after a trauma or crisis of some sort.

In any case, needless to say, our curiosity was building. It was a mixed blessing when we received our answer.

November 22, 2008

A turning point for all of us. We had been living in the house now for two months. It was a cool but pleasant late autumn day. Rachel and I were returning home from shopping at about 6:15 PM. It had just turned dark. We pulled up to the deck on the kitchen side of the house, which is next to miles of forest, and got out of the van. Both dogs ran to greet us as they always do. All of a sudden, they began to bark while running down the driveway into the backyard, which is bordered by forest on three sides. They ran to the bottom of the hill on the right side of the backyard.

Then we heard a sound that we'd never heard before. It was a very loud scream, approximately 30 feet from where we were standing. The scream was a cross between a woman, a cougar, and an ape. It was followed by four distinctive deep primate-type guttural sounds. The dogs came running back immediately.

Rachel and I looked at each other, and together both of us said "Bigfoot!" We were not frightened, but had a great peace on us. At that moment, we went inside to tell everyone else what had just happened.

Let me take a minute here to explain the behavior of our dogs. As mentioned before, they are two female Border Collie mixes. Sophie is about nine years old and has never been afraid of anything. I've seen her hold her ground while barking at two large bears, even when they both charged at her. She's been fearless even in the face of cougars. In fact, she loves to chase bears and coyotes. Molly is about four years old, is a bit more timid when she's by herself, but much bolder when she's with Sophie. While we lived on the coast, the behavior of both drastically changed, particularly at night. Molly has always been a wanderer, taking off down the road or into the woods in the past, but now she dawdled around the doors of the house, especially the sliding glass door off the kitchen leading to the deck. She used to love her doghouse, but now insisted on sleeping under a shelf on the corner of the deck under the kitchen window. Apparently she had a better view of her surroundings from there.

As soon as the sun went down, Sophie would want to come into the house. She has slept in the house at night for many years because when left outside, she would sit and growl or bark all night long, keeping us awake. But now, many, many times, day or night, if the dogs heard noises and gave chase, they would quickly return and run under the deck or the house. So as you can see, something was frightening them, unlike their past experience with animals and people.

Meanwhile, Rachel and I began to search out Bigfoot information on the internet. We listened to a few sound bites of purported Bigfoot vocalizations, and many of them sounded like the scream we had just heard, while other recordings matched some of the other sounds we had been hearing. Similar recordings of purported Sasquatch sounds can be heard at websites such as www.Bigfootsounds.com, www.bfro.com, www.OregonBigfoot.com, and www.Bigfootlives.com, just to name a few. As we continued to find out about the personality characteristics of these Bigfoot creatures and to read the testimony of other people who had had sightings, what we were experiencing began to make more sense. There are several very good and informative websites on the internet containing a wide range of Bigfoot information, including the websites mentioned above.

The next afternoon, my husband went and stood facing the forest on the deck outside the kitchen and let out a loud, very male, ape-like roar. Immediately, there was whooping and screaming coming from the forest sounding just like his roar. He did this four times, and each time received the same response. I didn't hear this exchange because I was in the office, but Rachel heard it all while in her bedroom with the windows open. She came running down to the office wide-eyed and excited to tell me what had happened.

We went to the computer and emailed a couple of Bigfoot groups and organizations. We never received any reply, except for one email saying, "If you're still having some activity in March when the weather breaks, please let me know then." It was November 23rd. We needed some answers right then.

Remember, we had been and were now definitely having our daily lives affected by strange and frightening situations. We began to believe we had real-life "Wookies," large Forest People living around us. What else could it be? So not knowing what else to do, we continued to search the internet for anything and everything about Bigfoot. We also began to listen outside carefully and note the sounds we were hearing. Our everyday lives were being affected by foreign and peculiar happenings. We could not really comprehend or explain the situation we found ourselves in. Not knowing what else to do, we continued to search the internet for something, anything that might help us unravel the mystery of these abnormal occurrences. Thus began our quest for clarification, and the start of our own research. We began familiarizing ourselves with the "normal" sounds and signs of a Sasquatch, as well as the subjective feelings their presence engendered. We commenced a journey of discovery, learning to record every little thing that was out of the ordinary.

December 22

Three days before Christmas, Elizabeth and Rachel stepped out onto the deck, bringing the dogs out of the house with them. Immediately, the dogs barked and ran up the hill, but then came running back down very quickly. The girls smelled a "wet, earthy, musty smell," and heard clear, distinctive grunts and footsteps running up the hill where the dogs had gone. This happened in the trees only about 15 feet from the deck.

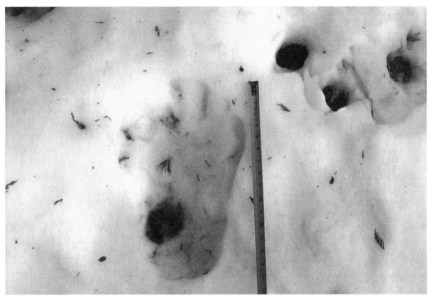

Figure 6: Track from December 22.

That evening it snowed. The next morning, Wayne, Elizabeth, and Rachel found three sets of Bigfoot tracks in the snow going up the hill on the side of the house. There were some good footprints among the tracks: Wayne took some pictures and measured some of them. They measured 16" long and 7" wide. We didn't know at the time that we should also have measured the depth of the print and how long the stride was from print to print.

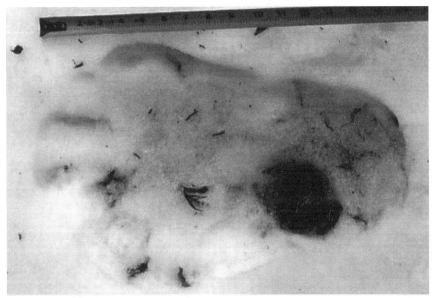

Figure 7: Closer view of December 22nd track.

Because the activity was increasing, on Christmas Eve we all decided that we really needed help from someone who knew more about what might be going on and how to deal with these creatures. We sent an email to another group of local investigators.

December 26

The day after Christmas, a local field investigator, who I will just call "Joe" (not his real name), called and asked permission to come over. He came with several other guys in trucks. They questioned us at length on all the details of our experiences and assured us we were not crazy. We were also told of some other sightings by people in that same area. After we were done talking to them, the group took off hiking around to see what they could find. They saw some footprints, but the snow had begun to melt off already, so they weren't as fresh as they had been earlier in the day.

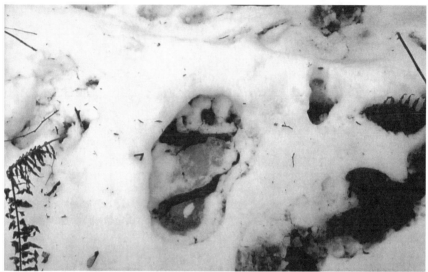

Figure 8: Tracks as the Bigfoot researchers saw them December 26.

Figure 9: Another track on December 26.

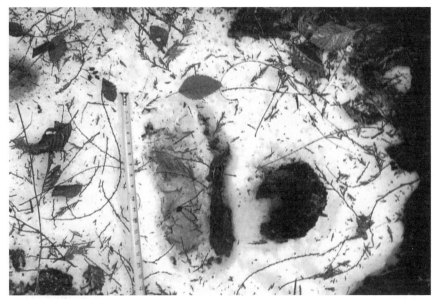

Figure 10: More track photos from December 26.

December 27

There was more new snowfall. That morning, we found more footprints in the backyard and along the tree line on the office side of the house, which is opposite the kitchen side. We called Joe the investigator, and he came out with his group to look around again. Before they arrived, Wayne and the girls did some hiking around themselves. They found some more tracks, took pictures, and even found a shelter of sorts in the meadow. The shelter was made of large branches bent over from trees, with others laid across the top. It had openings on either side. Next to it was a hole that was about 4 feet x 3 feet x 3 feet, not big enough for a Bigfoot, but perhaps they had just begun to dig and it was not yet completed.

December 31ˢᵗ

New Year's Eve. Darkness comes early this time of year, but late in the afternoon, Joe showed up with several cars full of guys and one woman named Barb. She was a local and fearless Bigfoot enthusiast who walked the woods at night, sometimes by herself. She had had several sightings of the creature, had been pelted with small rocks thrown by them, and had had many other experiences. Another woman once told her that her horse had its mane mysteriously braided by a purported Bigfoot while it was out at night in its corral.

Anyway, most of the men were "seasoned" Bigfoot researchers, we were told, although a few were not believers in the creature; some had even come from other states for the adventure on our property. They hiked around the place and deep into the surrounding forestlands for several hours until after dark. At that point, one man hit a tree trunk with a large stick several times to see if he would get any response. None came. Then they blew a horn, a very loud horn, and immediately a response came directly across the street from our house. It was a loud howl that repeated its cries for several minutes. It sounded wolf-like, and the men began to debate whether it was a wolf, a coyote, or a Bigfoot. It wasn't until several weeks later that I found out that the howling had been recorded and analyzed by experienced investigators. Apparently, according to the particular frequency of the sound, it was neither a wolf nor a coyote, leaving a possible conclusion that it was then most likely the cry of a Sasquatch in response to the horn blowing. Further along in this story, you will read that that same howling happened several more times in that same area.

Earlier in the day, the research group had set up eight cameras in various places on the property. These cameras were top of the line. They were the Reconyx-RC60-HO infrared, which snaps pictures day or night. They cost three times as much as the typical trail camera at Wal-Mart, but they have the shortest delay of any camera, will shoot one photo per second, and the motion-sensor's field of view is wider than the whole image, so it senses animal movement even before the animal is fully in the picture, giving you a much better picture.

Having Bigfoot in your backyard and other areas surrounding your home is like living in the Twilight Zone. Everything you do, outside in particular, is done with the thought that these creatures are or could be around and watching. We had to keep a constant watch on our granddaughter Lilee in particular, just because of our uncertainty regarding Bigfoot behaviour. It is our belief that they are simply curious about humans; at least, some of them are. This kind will sometimes approach humans, BUT ONLY ON THEIR TERMS! We have learned this from our own experiences and also from testimony of other long-term witnesses.

We also believe that there are indeed dangerous Bigfoot who can and do kill people.

Our daily lives became a routine of checking for tracks in the immediate yard; hiking into new areas for other evidence of possible Bigfoot activity; taking pictures; listening for sounds, calls, and other vocalizations and comparing them to audios and videos on websites; reading Bigfoot books and every tidbit of information we could find on the internet. As I mentioned, we would sit on the balcony at night with our night vision scope watching, listening, singing, calling, whistling, and so on. It would not be unusual for me to be awake and walking around the house in the middle of the night, checking the door locks, listening, and looking out of the windows. Insomnia is a terrible thing.

"Squatching," as going out looking for Bigfoot is called, does become a sort of addiction. The more you do and learn, the more you want to do and learn.

We began to share our experiences with some close friends, and yes, family. Why are families, of all people, the hardest to convince? At first they just laughed and mocked a bit, but after months of stories, having scrutinized the pictures we shared with them, most of them finally started to believe us.

2. THE JOURNAL

The text for this chapter comes mostly from the journal I began to keep some time in November. Because of the unusual circumstances we were experiencing, I thought that keeping a record of the events might be useful one day.

January 2

Joe returns and checks all eight cameras for any pictures. None were taken, so he decides to take four cameras back and leave only four.

January 4

A nice overcast Sunday afternoon, I hear two short teakettle/skill-saw screams across the street.

January 5

Joe returns to wipe new snowfall off the cameras. Up at the meadow, Joe finds great sets of footprints with four-foot strides. Of course, a trail camera was set up there.

Meanwhile, earlier in the day, Wayne was hundreds of yards from the house on the steep, grassy road that goes up to the meadow above the house. Near the top of the road, almost to the meadow, he leaned over to pick up a larch cone, and behind a big evergreen tree on the side of the road he heard a large branch break, and a skunk smell was projected towards him momentarily. He looked around but saw and heard nothing after that.

The girls had also been up in the meadow earlier in the day when they had also heard the breaking of big branches. They were walking through the other side of the meadow from where Joe would find tracks later on in the day.

Later that night, Wayne and I hear "whoooing," but it wasn't an owl. A short time later, I was on the balcony outside the dining room, when I heard something walking heavily and breaking branches. I ran to get Wayne and the night scope, but at the angle we were at, we couldn't see anything in the woods. [If I had been braver at the time, I would've gone right out on the deck outside the kitchen near where the noise was coming from.] They were either very loud or very close…or both. It was frightening. Molly the dog is so scared that she is scratching, pushing, and whining at the house doors, and at the office door.

January 6

Joe returns with a woman who I will call Barb and another guy whose name I have forgotten. They put up more trail cameras, then go hiking out in the woods up the hill behind the house, where there are acres of land owned by a lumber company. While out there, they ran across an older man who says he walks in the woods almost every day. Joe was honest with him about who they were and what they were looking for. The man says he hears strange screams at night from his house, which borders the other side of these woods from our house.

That night we hear screams and whistles.

January 9

Joe calls and says others have confirmed the authenticity of the pictures of the four-foot strides of footprints taken up at the meadow.

They will not be published anywhere yet because the location needs to be kept secret due to the ongoing investigation. [Update: The pictures are now on the internet at a Bigfoot website (can't give specifics) but the exact location where the picture was taken is still a secret.]

January 12

The girls were singing and vocalizing on the balcony tonight as usual. They received about eight yells back in response.

A short time later, as I was walking from the office to our bedroom door, the dogs came barking and running from around the other side of the house straight to the opposite side of the goat shed. I heard a loud growl and called the dogs. I grabbed a flashlight, but of course at that very moment, it was almost dead and needed to be charged. (Never fails!) I don't get a good look at what they were barking at. [If that situation happened today, I would be very tempted and might even run down to the shed where I heard the growl. I guess because of the knowledge I have obtained over this past year of living among the Forest People, I feel I am not as afraid as I used to be.]

Earlier that day, I noticed that the mulch pile, which we had just begun a few days earlier behind the shed and chicken coop, had been gotten into, and that several of the pumpkins were gone. The growl had come from that same area.

January 14

The girls and I notice that more pumpkins are gone from the mulch pile, and that the gate of the chicken coop (no chickens in the coop) had one hinge off and was halfway down on the ground like it had been pushed down.

January 16

Wayne and Rachel hear several screams off in the distance.

January 17

Rachel and I hike up the road to the meadow and catch a trail that leads to the logging roadway behind the house. We hiked quite a while, and then wound up circling around and again hitting the main road that runs in front of the house. While we were down there (it's kind of a valley back there), Rachel whooped twice and received a whoop back both times. We thought that it probably was just Elizabeth back at the house, but when we returned and questioned her, she said she had been in the house the entire time and hadn't heard a thing.

January 19

Today was very unusual. We have had very thick fog for several days now. Joe and another man actually got lost at night in the woods behind our house (where Rachel and I were just a couple of days ago), despite the fact that they were seasoned woodsmen and had a compass. We had to honk the car horn and bang on pots and pans after they called us on their cell phone until they found their way out. That's how foggy it was.

Shortly after they left, Wayne saw a pair of amber eyes piercing out from behind the goat shed. The next day, when he measured the approximate height of where the eyes had been, it was at around nine feet high.

About three or four hours later, as the girls were busy with their evening routine of singing and vocalizing on the balcony, they heard a two-footed creature walking near the goat shed accompanied by sounds that resembled a large stick being dragged against the building. They then heard a vocal grunt and more walking.

At 12:40 AM, Wayne stepped out of the office and walked toward the bedroom sliding glass door, approximately 20 steps. There was much fog at this time. The light on the deck on the other side of the house was shining down a ways into the backyard. Wayne stopped on the way just to observe the outside, as is his custom. Suddenly, in the outskirts of the light that shines down about 20 yards into the backyard from the deck on

Figure 11: The location where Wayne saw the Bigfoot walking across the lawn and up the hill. Balcony is on the left.

the other side of the house, Wayne saw a Bigfoot casually walking across the backyard towards the woods behind the house. The Bigfoot was walking just on the edge of where the shining light ends. Wayne saw the Bigfoot's right side from the waist down, just enough light catching its leg to make it visible. This creature appeared to have legs that were only around four feet long, so it might've been a juvenile. Wayne came and woke me up.

We went outside on the upper balcony to look and listen, but all was quiet. I went back to bed. A few minutes later (of course!), Molly began to bark quite intensely. I ran back upstairs, opened the sliding glass door to the deck off of the kitchen, and told Molly to "go get it." She gave me a look like "no way," ran the opposite way, and went to and hide under the deck. The rest of the night was peculiarly quiet.

January 20

A very foggy day and night. Joe arrives. Definite footprints are found in the backyard. No pictures were taken. The fog had created a frosty dew on the lawn, so the footprints showed up well. The trail cameras are moved again to the middle of the backyard facing the center of the yard, and more fruit is set out. Steelhead fish and fruit were also placed up in the meadow.

Before dark, big and loud bipedal walking is heard going up the hill near the back deck. Elizabeth hears it well, because she is on the balcony. The dogs run up the hill and immediately come right back down. Molly runs under the house and Sophie runs whimpering to the other side of the house. After a few minutes, the noises stop.

Later that evening, between 9:00 and 10:00 PM, while the girls were on the balcony, they again hear bipedal walking on the ridge of the hill behind the house. They search with a flashlight back and forth to see if they can see anything, and spot two amber-colored eyes peeking out from behind a tree located about eight feet from the part of the driveway that is between the house and the back woods. The flashlight kept dimming on and off.

The tree is located about six feet up the hill right above the area where Wayne had seen the Bigfoot two nights before casually walking across the backyard.

Immediately after the girls see the eyes, there is a definite wood knock on the other (west) side of the house, very close.

Figure 12: The balcony on the right is where the girls were standing when they saw the amber eyes between the branches of the tree located on the left of the picture.

January 21

Joe arrives, and after being told of the previous night's events, immediately goes to the tree where the eyes were seen. He finds five good hair samples, which he collects to be sent in for analysis. He also notices that two areas of moss on the tree were mashed down where it looked like something had been leaning on it (Bigfoot's arms?). A camera is set up in that area.

Later on that evening, Joe called and said that the camera in the pinecone pile near the bonfire pit in the backyard had snapped a picture of Bigfoot. It had been very foggy the night before, but the picture had some definite features and details.

[Unfortunately, we cannot print the picture because it belongs to the group of investigators, and we do not have permission to print it. Besides, the picture needs a verbal explanation in order to pick out the Bigfoot's image in the heavy fog. However, I will attempt to describe it: Just right of the center of the picture toward the top, an ape-like face with bared teeth (no fangs) is obvious, along with round eyes and a flat, wide nose. It has a cone-shaped to roundish head with no noticeable neck sitting on broad shoulders, long arms, and distinct abdominal and chest muscles. You can see the top of the legs, but nothing from the knees down. Again, if it were not for the severity of the fog, we would've had a remarkable photo of a Bigfoot.]

We were disappointed on one hand, but we knew that something had triggered the camera. Tricky little... well, big things! Joe, Barb, and some others come over and go hiking through the swampy area that is located up the hill behind the meadow. They don't find anything worth noting.

Later that evening before dark, there was some loud breaking of branches in the trees up the hill behind the house. The dogs ran up, but came back down right away. Molly went right under the porch. As I was outside checking out that situation and walking around, I found some really good footprints near a tree on the opposite side of the house near the chicken coop. We tarped the area so we could show it to Joe when he came a day or two later. Unfortunately, we didn't take a picture with the camera.

January 24

Joe had a friend who is a Bigfoot researcher and enthusiast. We thought he might be interested in what was going on at our place, so we emailed him and asked him if he'd like to take over our lease for the last six months. He replied that he was very interested indeed.

[Even though we were fascinated by the Bigfoot activity all around us, we still were not happy with the general area we lived in. Because of this, we began to reconsider a move to Oregon. Don't think we were thrilled about the prospect of another move, we weren't. Remember, we had only been in this house for four months. Moving a family of five plus animals is not easy, and I for one was tired, but a rare opportunity was right before us, and we took it.]

January 27

Barb comes over to spend a couple of nights. She and Elizabeth go down the road to a small, local state park to check out some areas that had broken branches. Branches that are broken or twisted high up in trees are sometimes a good indication of Sasquatch activity in an area. Although they did find broken branches and some other possible stick formations, nothing was certain.

January 28

Barb and the girls go hiking at another close-by state park; this one is larger and in an extremely dense rainforest environment. They hike down to the ocean. As they are walking along the beach, they hear something walking loudly and consistently parallel to their path in the forest, although they never get to see anything.

January 31

It's been pretty quiet lately, but we have this feeling that the Bigfoot are back in the neighborhood and on the property.

As the girls are out on the balcony for their evening routine of singing and vocalizations (whooping, whistling, etc.), they hear several rock knocks. They respond and then receive responses back. This was followed by many other sounds and vocalizations coming from several directions, including a seal-like sound.

We called Joe and he came out at around 1:00 AM. He also heard the sounds and the responses they were getting. At first, he was baffled by the different sounds he was hearing, especially the seal-like sound.

About an hour after he had left, he drove about half a mile down the road to a cove area, and actually saw a seal in the water making seal noises.

[Forest sounds can be confusing at times because they can vary according to wind, moisture, trees, terrain, elevation, and other factors. There are so many things that can alter the volume, direction, and distance of the sounds you are hearing that it's difficult to determine exactly where they are coming from some of the time.]

February 2

Barb is over again. She and the girls light a big bonfire in the backyard. They hear some noises and have feelings of being watched. Then come some definite rock knocks. Rachel plays a mixture of Bigfoot vocalizations she's recorded from several websites on the internet. Suddenly they hear a loud scream that turns into monkey-like chatter, and finally into a bit of a "Squatch talk" sounding rather like Japanese. Barb runs down the driveway hoping to find the original location. It sounded very close, possibly right across the street. She doesn't hear any more or see anything. They all decide to take a nighttime walk. It's a very cool and clear night, and they return without any new discoveries.

At 2:00 AM, Wayne and I are standing outside of our bedroom door on the porch, when we hear a couple of clear, distinctive, mournful cries coming from across the street in the woods at the same general location where we'd heard the wolf-like sounds. We've never heard anything like it before or since in our lives. It was a deep grieving sound, very emotional, very moving. We could almost feel it in our own bodies, if that makes any sense. This is the one and only time we have ever heard or felt anything like this.

February 4

Elizabeth and Rachel decide to take a walk in the backyard at night. They pass the goat shed and start walking toward the gate at the far end of the backyard from the house. All of a sudden, they have to stop because it's like they "hit a wall" and can't go any farther. Rachel has a really strong kind of surreal feeling and she hears words in her mind that say, "That's close enough. Don't come any closer." They turn around and walk back toward the house. They have that "feeling" of being watched. [Please be sure to read more about telepathic mind-talk that these Bigfoot creatures seem to use in the Research chapter.]

February 5

Lots of singing, rock knocking, wood knocking, and whooping by Elizabeth and Rachel, along with Lilee laughing and playing, results in lots of heavy bipedal walking up on the ridgeline of the hill behind the house. It always amazes me how these big guys walk so loudly and heavily one minute, and then you can't hear them walking at all the next.

Joe had come earlier and placed several cameras along the game trail on the ridge of the hill behind the house. Would we finally get some good pictures?

February 6

The girls find at least ten tracks up on the ridge, but this time Bigfoot had avoided the game trails where the cameras had been placed yesterday, and instead had walked through the brush. (Smart group!) Several more hair samples were found, collected, and sent off for analysis.

That evening we hear some definite rock knocks.

[Over and over again, the Bigfoot avoided the cameras, no matter where they were placed. This strange event happens all across the country and I'm sure in other places around the world to most researchers when they put out their cameras.]

February 7

Heard a couple of rock knocks during the day.

We found a dead, whole, uneaten bird on the ground lying next to the gate on the other side of the backyard from the house, right near the place where we had set out apples, pumpkins, and other goodies for our new friends.

[It has been reported several times before in habitation situations where humans leave gifts or food, that the Bigfoot, on rare occasions, may leave gifts of food in return. Was the dead bird a gift to us? I won't speculate. Let me also mention that there were three cats on the property at this time who loved to eat birds.]

February 8

Barb spent the night. Around midnight, she and I were outside whooping, whistling, and howling when we received some responses from directly across the street. First it was a kind of whooo, like an owl, and then it turned into a canine-sounding, howling screech! We've never heard a sound like that before.

The next response, a few minutes later, was also across the street but in a different location. It sounded like monkey chatter, clear as a bell.

February 9

It was one of those unusual, very quiet, eerie nights. [Remember, forests almost always have some kind of sound, whether it's from insects, animals, wind blowing through the trees, or moisture dripping form branches or bushes… things out there are alive and active. When it becomes nearly silent, something else is happening — a predator is present.]

February 10

Today is my birthday and it snowed all day long, about 6 inches.

Joe showed up with six or so people to go hiking. Elizabeth, with Lilee in a back harness, joined them. They were gone for a couple of hours and returned cold and exhausted with a report that they'd only found some tracks under thick tree coverage where there was little snow, but no fresh snow tracks.

[This particular winter was one for the record books as far as snowfall went. We thought moving to the coast would save us from large amounts of snow on the ground, as we'd been assured by the locals, but we all were wrong. At one point, for several days we couldn't even get out of our driveway because our neighborhood was last on the list for having our streets plowed. At the same time, we were actually land-locked because you couldn't drive north or south on I-5, the main freeway, and every pass over the Cascade Mountains going east was closed for days. Of course, to the west was the ocean, so, there we were, not liking the cut-off feeling whatsoever!]

February 11-28

This entry is being written after the actual dates. The last few weeks have been very, very busy around here, but I wanted to update a bit at this point.

Some observations: Since we've heard a type of monkey chatter on several occasions, we were told that certain woodpeckers and owls, particularly the barred owl, can make a monkey-like sound. We listened to several recordings on various internet sites. Even though some of them did indeed sound monkey-like, we do not believe it was what we had been hearing, although we had heard owls at night hooting sometimes.

[The concern about being long-term witnesses is to avoid calling every snap of a branch, howl, or noise a Bigfoot. On the other hand, long-term witnesses who live closely day-by-day with these creatures are not stupid people and should be given more credit by "researchers" than they are given. We would urge all those who are involved in this kind of situation to be extremely careful who you talk to about what's going on in your backyard. There are a few people that we have come to respect and regard as "safe" in this field. Autumn Williams of www.OregonBigfoot.com, who has had similar experiences in her own family as a child and is now a witness advocate, is on the top of our (short) list.]

One evening after dark, a creature across the street began to howl very loudly. We ran out onto the balcony and began to tape it. Despite the fact that a type of barking sometimes preceded the howling, it did not sound like a coyote. Coyotes usually travel in packs, they "yip," and whenever one starts yipping, they all seem to carry on in a chorus of insanity!

This was a lone creature. It howled a good thirty or so times, went quiet for about thirty minutes, and then started up again. It did this three times. It never seemed to move, but sounded like it stayed in the same area. Could it have been a wolf? I didn't know whether wolves were anywhere in the area. Also, the recordings of wolf howls I've heard seemed much lower-pitched.

Lastly, the howling came from the same area across the street where we've heard countless vocalizations over the last several months. This also seemed like a very good spot for them to observe us in the top floor of the house through the big windows, in the office, outside the office, front door, door to our bedroom, and all along the street side of the house.

When Joe heard the recording the next day, it was his opinion that it sounded identical to that which was heard and recorded back in December on New Year's Eve after a horn was intentionally blown by an investigator when a group of them were here.

One evening, the girls were taking the garbage out of the kitchen to the garbage can next to the garage. It would be taken out to the street for pickup in a few days. They walked out to the deck outside the kitchen and were about to go down the stairs to the garbage can (the house is tri-level), when they immediately felt and heard something. It was making a sort of chomping sound with its mouth. Instead of continuing on, they sat down on the edge of the deck and began talking and singing to it. The chomping stopped. After 15 or 20 minutes, they got up and finished taking out the garbage. The next morning, the garbage can was tipped over and the bag they had brought out was ripped apart, trash everywhere. Rachel's bedroom window is right above the area, and she said she heard something going through the trash. Was it a Bigfoot or the dog? Who knows? But Molly the dog hasn't gotten into the garbage before that night or since, and Sophie, the other dog, was in the house.

One last thing I failed to mention is that there have been many other sightings within just a few miles of our house over a period of a couple of years. Joe told us about a few of them the first day he and the other guys came to the house, but we began to hear more stories as the months went by.

A man driving down the road one night saw a large male Bigfoot at a gravel pit about a quarter mile from our house. Often, reports across the nation have come in about sightings at gravel pits. Do they need some kind of mineral in their diets that the gravel provides? Or does a gravel pit, being an open area, give the big guys some open space away from the enclosed thickness and darkness of the forest? Of course, no one is quite sure yet.

Two men were driving late at night and a Bigfoot crossed the road in front of them

Just down the street in broad daylight, a woman saw a Bigfoot standing at the tree line of her backyard, and she was also in the backyard. She quickly went into the house. From that point on, she tried to persuade her husband to move away from the area.

A teenager was home alone one evening when something looked in the window at him. His dog had been barking and acting strangely.

Several other reports of screams and other unidentifiable vocalizations have been reported.

Here is another incident — a "chance" meeting. One day after Joe left our place, he decided he was just going to drive around the area to look for signs of anything unusual. He made it about a half mile down the road, where there was a young woman hitchhiking. He picked her up in front of her trailer house. About ten miles down the road to her brother's house, he simply asked her if there was anything strange that had happened around the area in which she lived. She whipped her head around quickly and gave him a funny look. "Why, yes, there actually has been," she said. And she went on to say that she and her housemate always feel like they are being watched. They wondered why there are "people" walking in the woods at night. The housemate has insomnia quite a bit, so she's outside smoking her cigarettes at 2:00 or 3:00 in the morning, and hears all this walking going on. (Maybe some Bigfoot were trying to get the goats that were fenced up right next to the trailer house. That would make a nice dinner.)

Joe never said a word about Bigfoot, but what an interesting chance meeting that was!

3. THE LAST MONTH AND BEYOND

March was the last month we stayed at this home. As you can imagine, it was a very busy and stressful time, with all of the planning and packing.

As I sat and reflected on the last six months of our lives, and all of the changes it had brought, the reality of leaving became a bittersweet one. We all admitted that we were going to really miss the big guys (and gals).

I was even much too busy to write in my journal. There are a few highlights I do remember, and will mention here.

About the second week of March, I put up a "gift tree." I had read about something like it on the internet, and thought that we would give it a try. I found a large, broken, decaying trunk of a tree up the hill on the east side of the house. I placed fresh fruit, vegetables, chocolate candy, a baby doll (naked, with big eyes whose eyelids opened and closed), a long shining gold kid's necklace, and a continuous rotation of meat leftovers.

We told Joe that we did not want any cameras near the gift tree. On occasion, some food was eaten from the tree, but we couldn't determine which critter ate it, and nothing else was touched. We might have gotten better results had we been there longer.

Two weeks before we left, Wayne told Joe to remove all of the cameras from the property. My husband is an outdoorsman, and I didn't realize how confined he had felt with cameras mounted all over the property. We really never knew exactly where most of them were at any given time because they were constantly being moved around by the researchers.

Personally, I wish I could have spent more time outside hiking through the woods, although I did do some. But I was having some serious health issues on and off while we were there and I simply did not have the strength, so I wrote down everything instead. I did join the girls many evenings on the balcony for the singing and vocalizations. I'm glad to say I am much better now.

The activity was decreasing that last month, but there were times when they were around. After the cameras were all removed, there was more freedom in the air. I guess that is the best way to describe it. If we all felt a definite change, I wonder if the Bigfoot could feel it, too.

An amazing thing happened on our last day there. I don't call it a coincidence, because I don't believe in that. Things just don't happen by chance, but are a part of an overall plan.

We were all packing up the U-Haul truck, van, and pickup truck on the driveway, which is parallel to the street in front of the house. All of a sudden, loud howling came from across the street, as we had heard many times before, but usually at night. It was a strange moment, and hard to describe because it was one of those surreal moments. We all looked at each other and said, "He is saying good-bye to us." I actually kind of got choked up. We said good-bye back to him.

Staying there at that time was our new friend Barb, who was coming to live in the house for the next six months to continue the research. We have remained in contact with her all this time. She has told us that there has been very little Bigfoot activity at the house and surrounding area since we left.

The most dramatic and definite thing that did happen, though, was one evening when Barb and a lady-friend of hers were sitting on the deck talking and laughing. Barb went into the house and downstairs to the place that used to be our bedroom. Suddenly, she heard a very loud and deep *SIGHHHH* coming from what seemed like the side of the house under the balcony. She ran back upstairs and asked her friend if she had heard the noise, which she had. She described it just as Barb had heard it. We joke with her that it must have been a male Bigfoot who was watching them and frustrated, realizing he couldn't have either one of them to add to his female harem.

No pictures have been taken, despite the fact that many cameras were put back up on the property, and also some others across the street. A feeding station that remained stocked with all sorts of food that would appeal to a Bigfoot was set up with a camera 24/7, but still no pictures, although food disappeared at times. Only an animal that was tall could have reached it, for it was set up at about eight feet high. A funny story, at least I think so, is that the cameras were mysteriously and suddenly turned off one day and turned back on three days later… and the food was gone. The camera actually records the time and other kinds of information. There were no people around in the area of the food station. Did the Bigfoot do this?

Barb told us that despite all the time she spent there, she never heard any howling like we had experienced during our stay. The whole research project was shut down in September 2009.

Update: The house was sold soon after that when the lease was up.

We have found out that the new owner was told about the Bigfoot activity. He was very excited, because supposedly he had experienced his own Bigfoot sighting back in the late 1970s. He is eager and willing to continue with the cameras, the feeding station, and other research activities on his new property and to work with the researchers.

The previous owner who we leased the house from was finally told by the researchers what went on during our stay and why we subleased the house for the last six months to the "other" people. Actually we had mentioned our initial experiences with Bigfoot to her, but it was very early on in our encounters with Bigfoot, so she wasn't convinced by us at the time. But when she was told, even she was excited to hear about the existence of Bigfoot. She stated that during the eight years that she lived there, she'd often felt that someone was watching her.

4. FROM THE REST OF THE FAMILY

Even though my family, my husband Wayne, Elizabeth the oldest daughter, and Rachel the youngest, had great input in helping to put this story together, it's important that you hear some of their experiences in their own words.

Wayne's Story

Wayne here, hi. Right before I get to the actual experiences I had with the Bigfoot folks, I'm including an overview of how for several decades, I had been walking down a path that introduced me to and made me acknowledge the actual presence of Bigfoot among us on this earth.

Up until the time I actually experienced Bigfoot, I never really considered that I would ever meet up with one, much less some of 'em. So, it was a big surprise to me the first time I actually saw one face to face: Then and there, I realized that I was entering a new dimension.

First, I remember back in the 1960s hearing of Bigfoot, most likely on TV, where they were showing a female Bigfoot that had been filmed over in California, the Patterson film. But still, I didn't think a lot about

Bigfoot at that time, especially since I figured that if they did exist, they were over in California and other places that had mountainous evergreen forests. So I focused on the more immediate things where I was at the time. Texas is known for having plenty of wild things to look out for, so I was kept busy there watching my steps.

My next hint of Bigfoot happened when I was driving over to northern New Mexico in the early 1970s. I was a hundred miles or so into the state, getting close to the Sangre de Christo Mountains, when, feeling okay about it, I picked up a tall Native American hitchhiker out in the middle of the open plains. Still, I initially had him ride in the back of my pickup truck. After we had stopped for a burger and fries in one of the small towns on the way, I decided that he seemed to be a safe enough person to ride up front. Sure enough, he was. He showed himself to be a friendly who was on his way back to Colorado Springs, getting back to some work he had in that area.

So as we sped down the road talking, the hitchhiker began telling me some of his earlier experiences that he had while living in his home state of Washington. These were experiences that took place up on Mount Rainier, where he liked to spend a lot of time. He revealed to me that being high up on that mountain, he actually saw a Bigfoot in the forest. I thought it was interesting, but it was still a remote concept for me, so even though I clearly remembered it, I didn't give it a lot of thought. I was mostly focused on my own time in the mountains of New Mexico.

Now, another thing of note that the hitchhiker told me, which has turned out to influence my present and recent perception of Bigfoot, is that while he had spent some time up on Mount Rainier, he'd come upon an older gray-haired man who was actually living high up on that mountain. He said that this man claimed to have been living on the mountain for the last five years. But what about the cold snow-filled winters up on that mountain? The man said that he would simply come down to lower elevations on the mountain where there was a cave to take shelter in.

The main thing that struck me concerning the man on the mountain, that has stuck in my mind for the thirty-five years since the hitchhiker mentioned him, was that when this man would walk out into the forest away from the campsite they were temporarily sharing, apparently being so in harmony with the flow of nature around him, he would virtually disappear. That is, the hitchhiker said that the man could blend so well into the forest around him that it was the same as disappearing, because the hitchhiker couldn't see him. The hitchhiker said that he'd also spent a lot of time in mountains and forests during his lifetime, so for this man on the mountain to vanish from the hitchhiker's sight, who was a person well experienced in forest living, I figure that was something to remember.

Now, because I knew that the man on the mountain blended in with his natural surroundings, it's clear to me why after spending literally years in the forest and mountains myself, I had never seen a Bigfoot (that I'm aware of), heard one, nor was ever conscious of any other kind of evidence of their presence out there in the wild.

I was only on guard for cougars, grizzlies, black bears, wolves, rattlesnakes, and dangerous humans. It never occurred to me to be looking out for the big hairies, until our six-month experience in the

Pacific Northwest coastal area. I believe if they'd wanted me to be aware of them, I would have seen them, but they were as stealthy as possible, blending into their surroundings.

Bigfoot's ability to blend into their surrounding so well, making them difficult for man to perceive them, pretty well explains an incident I had deep in the forest in Montana just four years or so before our Pacific Northwest encounters.

Far back in the mountain forests of northwest Montana was a place that, as far as I could tell, had next to no human visitors, even though I had actually gotten there by a gravel road. For those of you who have never spent much time in "outback" mountain regions, it is like that. There are various kinds of gravel roads back there, most of them rough and sketchy, but there hardly ever seems to be anyone traveling on them, at least where I have traveled. Those kinds of places definitely lack the feeling of a human presence.

Back to the story. I had just gotten out of my truck to scope out the area for some forest products, when I noticed that there was, I figure, about a ten-pound rock on the road that was near one of my truck tires. I realized that I needed to move the rock to prevent possibly hitting it with the tire later on when it was time to leave. So, I reached down to get the rock and threw it behind me away from the gravel road, I estimate about twenty feet.

Thing is, before I started to stand up straight again, that rock had come gently flying back to me, landing within just a couple of feet from where I was standing almost right where it had been before. I'm thinking, "Man, what's going on here?" I'm having this very unusual experience out there, deep in the woods, alone. I wasn't scared, just amazed and curious. I immediately turned around towards the direction that I had thrown the rock, the view being grass, bushes, and trees, but saw nothing that would explain what had just happened.

I looked for anything that could possibly have caused the rock to bounce back at me from the spot where it would have landed, but there were just some grasses that were about a foot tall, and absolutely nothing that could have caused the rock to bounce back to me. For about a minute, I continued to look in the direction where I'd thrown the rock, but saw nothing and no one.

So, barring even stranger possibilities for how that could have happened in the natural world and based on some personal knowledge I now have about Bigfoot, I now consider it a big possibility that there could have been one of them living in the area where this happened.

Judging by what I have observed of Bigfoot folks during my six months of living among them, they are playful and curious. So the "ten-pound rock" incident could have been a Bigfoot just playing around with a very infrequent human visitor or curious as to what I would do when the rock returned.

There was another incident on my path towards meeting the Bigfoot folks. This took place only about a year and a half before I actually met them. It happened on a 1,200-acre ranch in northeast Washington where we were living at the time. Looking back to a particular time at that ranch, I recall something that I had attributed to men. Now, I believe it was the Bigfoot folks. Some incidents occurred out in the wild around the house that one night. I first thought it was men out there trespassing, but after six months of observing Bigfoot on the coast, I now believe it was, sure enough, them and not men.

Here's what happened: In northeastern Washington at our ranch house, late on a moonlit night backed by thousands of wild acres of forested hills, I was in the house preparing to go take a look outside into those dark woods because that is just something I do on a regular basis. As I was opening the glass door, which was on the side of the house next to a fifty-foot slope down to a grassy area before the woods and hills, I heard what I now know was a Bigfoot "wood knock."

At the time, I believed the sound might be from some men that a neighbor told me were snooping around the forest within a few miles of the ranch and forestlands where we were living. We had heard that this neighbor came across these guys, who said they were part of a Homeland Security training camp up in the mountains behind our house. If that wood knock had been from them, they were being far from subtle about their presence when they saw me opening the sliding glass doors. I mean, it was very obvious. If they were to signal each other like that in a combat situation, they wouldn't last long, far as I can tell. As I am right now writing this, though, I realize that judging by my past experience with Bigfoot, knowing the sounds they make and how they make them, and from my encounters with them, they would in fact make those kinds of sounds in a human's presence without the caution a combatant might be trained to exercise.

About wood knocks: We think that Bigfoot uses wood knocks, the hitting together of tree branches of various sizes, as a means of signaling one other, or for other reasons yet to be revealed.

As soon as I looked out the sliding glass door into the dark, moonlit surroundings, I heard the hitting together of what sounded like two dry tree branches, each about four inches thick. This seemed to be a signal from one person to another about my presence. The sound happened at the very moment that I was opening the glass sliding door and looking out. Looking back, I believe that I most likely had a Bigfoot "wood knock" experience.

Another strong point is the fact that any people walking out in that wooded, grassy area behind our ranch house late at night would basically have some kind of death wish, considering the abundance and almost continual presence of grizzly bears, black bears, cougars, coyote packs, rattlesnakes, and other wild creatures we lived among.

I actually had a similar experience with the Bigfoot folk at our coastal house. One night, I opened the sliding glass door of our bedroom onto the patio, in clear view of the front forest and the side yard with forest on three sides of it, and stepped out. Immediately, a Bigfoot whistled with two short whistles as if signaling another. This reminded me of the wood knock I'd heard in eastern Washington.

In addition to our own experiences in eastern Washington, we have since heard of other Bigfoot sightings and evidence from the same forested mountainous areas where we were living.

Okay, so now that I have gone on about how I believe I was on the path to meet some Bigfoot folks, I will start relating what happened when we moved to the house in the Pacific Northwest coastal area.

There was a very thick-forested area all around our house and beyond. This densely forested area near our house had a definite "feel" to it that I now call the "Bigfoot presence" — very unusual.

Shortly after we moved into the house, Julie, Lilee, and I visited a nearby state park to go on a hike down to the shoreline of the Pacific Ocean. We hiked down a trail through very lush vegetation and trees for about a half mile to the shore. When we had walked about halfway to our destination, Julie and I said to one another, kidding, but sincere: "Bigfoot lives here." Little did we understand at that moment how correct that statement actually was, and how soon our lives and the way we viewed earthly nature around us were about to change.

When we had finished moving into the house and started settling in, I began noticing, both day and night, that the woods surrounding the house had an unusual quietness and that unusual "feel" that I didn't yet understand. Also, there were hardly ever any birds flying or singing in the neighboring woods, although I had seen and heard them in other nearby areas along the coast. Though we knew that deer and coyotes were around in abundance — for we saw deer and heard coyotes regularly at night — they usually kept their distance from our house, very unlike the wild animals in other wilderness areas we'd lived in.

A couple of months later, after we had found out that we were living among Bigfoot folks, we found out something that might cause the deer to keep their distance from our house. In the thick woods several hundred yards from the house we were living in, we came across an area where many deer carcasses and bones were lying fairly close together. It looked like someone's feeding ground, someone who fed on the abundance of deer. We didn't know of bears or cougars or any other animals that normally and consistently pile up deer remains in a single place like this, so we figured it must be the Bigfoot folks who were leaving all those deer remains in that area after they had killed and eaten 'em. Bigfoot tracks had also been seen in that same area, further supporting our conclusion that it was, in fact, a kind of restaurant for the big hairy forest people.

My first encounter with Bigfoot at the Pacific Coast house began after three days of living there. The time was around 10:00 PM, and I was outside on the patio, near the office door located at the lowest level of the residence. Suddenly, in the wooded area in front of me that runs between the house and street, I heard a heavy-sounding biped stomping on the ground as it walked through the thick bushes and trees, heading away from where I stood. I detected an attitude of frustration, judging from the way this person was walking and from what I heard it do next. Next came the sound of something fairly heavy being thrown across the bushes maybe 15 feet, and it seemed to me like what a 50-pound bale of hay would sound like if it was being thrown through the thick brush. I use hay as a reference, because I've had the pleasure of throwing bales of hay. Again, it sounded like whoever or whatever was throwing something across the bushes was frustrated. It seemed they were not pleased by our recent arrival at the residence.

We brought along two dogs, which the former resident of some years didn't have. Our dogs barked at strangers of any species and had many years of experience chasing most any forest creatures. During much of their lives, I've watched Sophie and Molly chase bears, cougars, coyotes, and bobcats.

Another observation regarding this first known encounter is that after the heavy walking and the heavy object being thrown across the bushes, everything in the surrounding area suddenly went silent. It was like listening to pure silence, silence designed to accentuate the previous heavy walking and throwing of the heavy object. The person doing this in the woods didn't make a sound that I could hear after this demonstration of frustration. I did not hear this person walk away, and I never saw him that night.

So, I read the behavior as a way of sending their message to me. Of course, this person in the woods could easily see me, and would know if I got the message, too.

Now because of the heavy sounding walking, and the heaviness of the sound of whatever had been thrown across the bushes, I figured that it could in fact be a Bigfoot. I didn't think it was a bear or a man because of the heavy-sounding bipedal walk, the throwing of a heavy object a good distance, and because whoever it was was walking through the trees and bushes in pitch black darkness without any hesitation, noting that all of the forest that we were living in was very rugged land. A human would almost always have to watch their step there. I also figured that a bear wouldn't have any reason to walk on its hind legs, especially doing it while walking away from me. I had simply stepped outside of the house to go to the office, without projecting any kind of threat. So, it wasn't making sense to me that it could be a bear, judging from my past experience with them.

Furthermore, I'd actually in the recent past witnessed a bear stand up and stare at me for a couple of minutes while I was on the Flathead River in northwest Montana. It turns out that he was just looking at me over the tall grass that was in front of him so that he could see me, and to determine whether I was going to leave the area any time soon. The place he wanted to go looked like a place with easy access to the river, a good place to drink, fish, and swim. So I had this incident in mind when trying to guess what kind of person was out there in the dark woods in front of my house sending me an "instant message."

Also in past bear observations, I never remember hearing bears make stomping noises when they walked on their hind legs. They seemed to walk much more quietly. Nor in any of my many encounters with bears in the Pacific Northwest lands did I ever see them pick up heavy objects and throw them in disgruntled response to my presence among them. They usually ignored me or ran away from me and my dogs.

And I never felt that the bears were frustrated when they came through our property at our other houses in the rural wild country. They were mostly just looking for something to eat, and just went on their way, as long as we kept our distance and didn't appear to threaten them.

So, I came to the conclusion that it was probably a Bigfoot out there sending me a message that he was frustrated. We later came to understand that if there were family-type messages to be communicated, it would be to me, the man of the house. That is their perception of the man, his house, and his family.

As time went on, it seemed that anything that happened that they didn't like was brought to my attention, almost always at night when I was in the office or outside near the office where they could easily communicate to me in their guarded way, usually without me being able to see them clearly.

They could easily see me through the big glass windows of the office as I sat at the desk. So, several key times when they wanted to express their displeasure to me, they would send what I came to understand as infrasound. This infrasound felt like small, gentle, harmless, lightning-like electrical jolts running vertically down the left side of my chest. It only happened once per night when they communicated with me. Somehow, I could also feel that they were displeased with something presently going on around the house or around one of their dwelling places way up on top of the hill behind the house, which we would discover later on.

There were a couple of times that they directed skunk scent at me. This scent would come from a definite direction, always in the dark, and it would last for only a few seconds. Must be why some call them Skunk Apes. I will say that their displeasure always seemed related to confrontations with the two dogs, the many cameras that had been placed in the woods around our house by Bigfoot researchers, or the occasional Bigfoot researchers who'd show up and hike through their home territory looking for them.

Something else that occurred to me is that even though I'd had the encounter mentioned above, I still didn't associate it with those weeks and months of being watched nightly while in the house. I don't remember ever considering that it might be Bigfoot. The house had big windows on the upper main floor for watching the forest during the day, and there were no curtains or other window coverings. So, we could easily be seen through those windows at night while we were in the kitchen, dining room, or living room.

I didn't attribute any of this to Bigfoot: the fact of their presence was still not sinking in. But soon I figured that if it had been a human lurking in the woods around the house, they would have had our two dogs on them immediately. The dogs, though, were not going after any lurkers outside.

Since then, we've learned that the dogs were greatly intimidated by Bigfoot, especially whenever there was a close encounter. Whoever it was outside looking into our house was not being chased down by the dogs. Rather, it was the dogs that were being found on a regular basis hiding under certain parts of the house or deck.

My next encounter with our new forest neighbors and the first time I saw one of them was late at night several weeks into our stay there. Everyone else had gone to sleep and I was still in the living room upstairs, sitting in a chair facing the back of the house where the forest goes on for miles without any houses or other buildings. The back porch light was still on, so when Molly (one of our dogs) came to the back sliding glass door with the curtains open, I was able to see her instantly. She seemed extremely frightened and intimidated, and desperately wanted to be let into the house. So, I got up and went out on the back deck to see what was going on out there to cause this kind of reaction in her. I stood there on the lit deck looking directly into the forest and up at the very dark hill as best I could. After a couple of minutes spent observing the surroundings, I saw and heard nothing; Molly just stood nearby looking like she hoped I would let her into the house when I went back in. What happened next was an entry into a new dimension.

As with the rest of my account of my experiences with our forest neighbors, I am just going to tell what I believe I saw while standing on that back deck, without going into a lot of explanation.

After checking the back of our house, I turned to go back inside, opening the sliding glass door. As soon as I began to turn around, I saw over in the bushes behind the house where the forest begins, about 25 feet away, a Bigfoot sitting down with his head turning towards me slowly as I also was turning. He had apparently had his hairy head turned away from me the whole time I had been standing out there to prevent me from seeing him.

But what helped to expose him, besides his large, dark, hairy head slightly showing in the porch light, was when he began to look directly at me with a "not friendly at all" look. As he turned fully towards me to watch me go into the house, his large right eye seemed to simultaneously remain in his body and also travel towards me through the air three quarters of the distance to where I was standing. With all of this happening in just a few seconds, as unusual as it was, I still proceeded to go into the house. I've had many unusual experiences in my lifetime, so I chalked this one up as just another one.

Judging by the size of this Bigfoot, I figure it was a male. I also figure it was male because of the way he looked at me as I went into the house. He looked at me in a way that wouldn't encourage me to consider ever being his friend, and in a way that showed he was not scared of me. Shortly after this encounter, I saw that Julie and the girls seemed to believe my account of what I had experienced, but some others who heard my story were skeptical, with a snickering look on their faces.

No problem, I know what I saw.

From that time on, I kept an eye out for evidence of these newfound neighbors. And sure enough, throughout the remaining months of our stay at that house, they made themselves known. At least three times, I saw their amber eyes glowing in the darkness of night as I was out on the front porch area. Once, one was near the sheds in the backyard looking around the back side of the shed at me. The next day, I measured the height of where I had seen the eyes — nine feet high.

Another time, I saw those amber eyes staring at me from the forest across the street in front of the house. This one was about twenty feet up a tree, just about level with me where I was standing on the front porch.

The third time I saw the amber eyes, they were fairly close to me by the front office. Bigfoot was just down the slope in front of the house in the darkness staring straight at me. The gaze from the amber eyes in the darkness was very different from the way that first Bigfoot had looked at me. Best way I can explain it is that there was a playfulness in those eyes, even a kind of goofy look. I saw no threat in those eyes, just someone having a fun time.

One other time I saw one of these forest folks, it was a very foggy night. I was out on the front porch facing the street, but the light on the back porch was on, sending light down towards the side yard. From that position, I had a good view of the side yard where I saw this Bigfoot. Without having my attention drawn by any sound, I saw a Bigfoot walking across the backyard, barely in that porch light, walking with much casualness towards the back forest area. From what I could tell, this one was maybe a female or juvenile because the length of its legs was only maybe four feet long. But what really stood out when I saw this one was the definitely casual demeanor with which it walked. Surely knowing I was there on the porch maybe 20 yards away, it strolled by as though it had no fear whatsoever of my presence.

As for hearing our forest neighbors, I have only a couple of tales to tell. One time, I was outside near the house. Across the street a couple of hundred yards into the forest, I heard what I can best describe as a skill-saw screeching sound. I say skill saw because when I was a carpenter, we used to call all circular saws skill saws. This skill-saw screeching was attended by three or four dogs barking, and it sounded like they must be in close proximity to each other.

What further convinced me that this was a Bigfoot was that in a minute or so, I heard this screeching again, but a couple of hundred yards down from where I'd first heard it. Again, there were more dogs down there barking along with this skill-saw screeching. And then further proof for me is Julie saying that she also heard this sound.

As for other Bigfoot sounds I heard, one day Julie was in the office on the computer checking out a Bigfoot website, listening to sounds someone had recorded of Bigfoot howls. I happened to come into the office and listened to these sounds also. After listening, I immediately went upstairs to the other side of the house on the back deck where I had first seen Bigfoot. Facing the hilly forest, I proceeded to yell out as close as possible what I had just heard on the recording. To my great surprise, I got an immediate response from a Bigfoot, actually over in the area where I had heard the skill-saw-like screeching yells before. I yelled out four times, mimicking what I'd heard on the recordings, and just like clockwork, I got four responses in kind from what seemed to be the same forest person over there in that same area of woods.

I went back inside the house and saw Rachel coming up the stairs with a surprised look on her face. She told me that she had just heard the same thing. So, there you go, I have a living human witness, to boot.

Another experience I would like to relate may seem "out there" to some of you, as if what I've already talked about isn't already "way out" in the minds of many folks. But like I said earlier, I'm just going to explain what happened during our short stay at that house and try to make my story understandable.

Because I enjoy making some music, I like to enter into the sounds almost daily on whatever the present instrument of choice is. At the time I'm referring to, it was a classical guitar. So one night, after finding out about our unusual neighbors in the forest, I was enjoying some sounds on the guitar. My common method of making sounds is with my eyes shut, which helps me concentrate on the actual music, rather than on the instrument. As I was listening to the music with my eyes shut, I suddenly had a telepathic image sent into my mind. In living color, a male Bigfoot with reddish brown hair, his image from the shoulders up, was looking at me with a friendly face and an interest in what I was doing.

This telepathic messaging from animals and other creatures wasn't new to me. In the past when I had parakeets living in another room of my house, a couple of times when they needed food or water, they sent their image into my mind. Sure enough, when I responded, mostly out of curiosity as to whether this was really a message from them, it turned out to be true. They did need food and water. I had this kind of experience with our dogs, also. Again it was a food issue: they sent their image into my mind, I went ahead and responded, and it turned out they needed some food.

So, I was prepared beforehand by these mental exchanges with parakeets and dogs to receive communications from other creatures. The Bigfoot male, it seemed, sent several messages like this to me in the months we lived there, as I enjoyed sounds on the guitar, and they were simply that he liked the music.

Still more evidence I had of our forest neighbors was finding one of their dwelling places. I say one, because as vast as that forest is, as stealthy as they seem to be, and knowing they are capable of traveling great distances if need be, they probably set up more than one place to shelter. That year, we happened to have an unusual snow on the coast of over 22 inches. We were told that the normal average snowfall in that area was around one inch a year, so 22 inches in a couple of days would also be something of a surprise for Bigfoot, I figure.

Turned out that after the snow fell one night, in the morning we found many Bigfoot footprints in our side yard close to where the sheds are, where the formerly used chicken shed was. Looked like Bigfoot was taken by surprise by the weather and didn't care about leaving prints in many parts of our yard in its quest for food.

I'm talking about prints of one of the bigger guys, footprints over 16 inches long.

This was a real surprise for all of us, so we were sure to get plenty of pictures of the footprints. We also went walking around the perimeter of the house looking for more prints and evidence. I went up the hill behind the house and began seeing occasional footprints heading up to the top of the hill.

Up on top of the hill, there is a clearing where mainly grasses grow. This meadow is somewhat circular in shape, with a diameter of about two hundred yards and a few interspersed trees. All around the edge of this meadow is dense forest. Along the edge of the meadow in the direction of our house is a long line of blackberry bushes. Along these blackberry bushes for about 175 yards I quickly discovered over 150 large Bigfoot footprints, all over 16 inches long.

There were other, smaller prints in a couple of other places, but I am focusing on only these large prints at this time. I followed these footprints along the blackberry bushes to where they ended at what looked like a shelter that had been built out of blackberry bush branches. This shelter was right on the edge of the meadow next to the forest. Because of the abundance of blackberry bushes around it, it blended in with the surroundings and wasn't obvious.

I spotted it at that time because I had followed the footprints right up to one of the entrances, and that is also where those footprints in the snow ended. It happens that around this shelter, there was hardly any snow on the ground, mostly because the trees and blackberry bushes prevented it from hitting the ground.

This blackberry bush shelter, which was about three hundred yards from our house, was about twenty feet long and consisted of, I estimate, fifteen-foot blackberry branches at right angles to the length, all bent over creating a domed roof. Holding the branches in place were several tree trunks about eight inches in diameter lying on top of the branches, and they were almost the same length as the shelter. The branches were bent over towards the trees of the forest and away from the meadow. This blackberry shelter had enough space inside to hold at least a couple of full-sized Bigfoot folks lying down. It had openings at both ends, each about the same size and big enough to allow a Bigfoot to enter. And one of the openings had a worn path right up to it starting at the meadow and continuing onward for about eight feet. This was the same place where the footprints I was following ended.

My last experience with Bigfoot at the house on the Washington coast was when we were getting ready to leave to go to our new location. It was in the morning, and we were all standing outside by the cars and trucks already packed and ready to go. Suddenly, across the street in the forest and in the location where many times we had heard their howling and other sounds, was a mournful cry and howl, as though this one was sad to see us go and was openly and honestly expressing itself. A very nice send-off from our short-term friends and neighbors.

Elizabeth's Story

Considering that I was not born and raised in the deep woods or the mountains, when I came to live with my family in the gorgeous Flathead Valley of Montana in 2003, I did not realize what an extreme change this would be for me. I had never been to the great northwest, had never seen or experienced the awe and majesty of mammoth mountain ranges or done any of the incredibly exhilarating snow sports or games such as sledding, skiing, snowball fights, and so on as a child because of my southern upbringing. So, here I was as a teenager coming from a school in Mississippi and going to the Big Sky Country to live on an Indian reservation near a national bison range and close to Glacier National Park. You can surely imagine the culture shock.

During the three years I resided in Montana, I fell in love with exploring the intricacies of nature. Every day, I felt drawn to the smell of pine needles and wildflowers, the sound and feel of mist from a roaring waterfall on my face, the flavor in my mouth, the adrenaline rush received by watching a herd of elk galloping through the forest. You know the saying that mountain air can and does heal a multitude of ailments... well, it is true. I became a free spirit and felt at peace whenever I was outside surrounded by God's creation.

Because our home was neatly situated in the foothills next to a mountain run-off stream that ran through our property, I was able to feed my craving by spending endless hours every day in the forest. Many times, I saw and stumbled across bears (among tons of other wildlife), that taught me to always be cautious and very observant of all my surroundings. I also enjoyed collecting things such as mushrooms, pinecones, flowers, bugs, plants, and herbs; through experience, I could look at a densely forested area and find what I was searching for. These skills would come in handy later on when I searched in other forests for things that seemed invisible and impossible to locate. I unfortunately do not recall hearing, sensing, or seeing anything that would lead me to assume the presence of Sasquatches during this time. Yet looking back, I wish I had known then what I do now, because encountering a habitation situation and having earlier contact with the cryptid would have been awesome.

Several years later, my sister Rachel, my daughter Lilee, and I had an opportunity to go up to Alaska to work for the summer. An entirely different realm of wilderness was now presented to me to explore and add to my list of adventures. There were sea creatures such as whales, seals, and crabs; wildlife such as Kodiak bears, bald eagles, and huge wolves; natural wonders such as unique icebergs from marvelous glaciers, turquoise waters that shimmered like diamonds, and rivers at low tide filled with hundreds of stranded fish making mazelike patterns in the earth in their attempts to get to more water.

I was exposed to many more of this world's wilderness wonders during my time in Alaska, and I believe I became increasingly sensitized to the structure and flow of nature. Everything has a specific purpose, a unique pattern to its life, and something special to contribute to nature's overall beauty. Having these ingrained beliefs, my thinking has been opened to vast mysteries and knowledge of the world that no person can fully understand or fully grasp.

It was as I listened to my dad's first attempt at imitating a Sasquatch call one evening and hearing the responses from somewhere out in the distance that I started to be inquisitive, compelled, and devoted to studying and searching for the truth about the legendary myth for myself. The sudden interest my family and I had to find out what was really out there during this quiet yet extremely intense season of our lives was the beginning of a lifelong passion for me: I yearned to discover and experience more of what I now cannot deny as genuine. After just a short time spent living in this totally new rainforest habitat teeming with life, we all witnessed to the fact that there was something disturbing and unsettling about the forest around our house, particularly at night.

The abnormal behavior of our dogs was our first clue that the creepiness we were all sensing was more than just feelings. We had not seen anyone or anything spying on us, but I can recall many times when I was in my bedroom at night reading or listening to music, and would suddenly stop and become attentive for some unknown reason. It was not frightening, nor did it cause me any anxiety. It was more like a penetrating spirit that caused me to be cautious and on guard. I always stopped what I was doing, got up, and walked over to look out the curtainless window facing the hill behind our house, anticipating or expecting whatever aroused such a disturbance within me to appear. If you have ever been imposed upon and completely not at peace in your own home — a place that is supposed to be a safe haven — you can easily understand my need to scrutinize every possible source of such bizarre feelings.

The internet was, of course, our first resource. After doing a search on all the known wildlife that inhabited the area and coming up with nothing, we began to broaden our search and seek unknown creatures. While reading modern accounts and others dating back hundreds of years from all over the world and from various geographic terrains, we began to see the connections with our own story. We became well informed about the character and behavior of a Bigfoot-type animal through descriptions from thousands of eyewitnesses and interactions throughout history, and by listening to a variety of recordings documented for scientific research, with no conclusive evidence as to the origin of the sounds. In addition, we became connected with certain research groups in the hope of having some of our questions as to the possibility that Sasquatches were watching us answered.

With no other way to resolve my bewilderment, I opted for the likelihood that there was indeed a human-like, ape-like creature, until I found sufficient evidence to convince me otherwise. Instead of listing all the different things about Bigfoot I learned through research that my mom has already recounted here, I would like to share how I used that information for my own daily routine of trials and results. I do need to mention two important points I did learn, though, for others to better understand my conclusions.

I learned that they've been known to make a variety of noises and behave in such purposeful ways in communicating with each other that the possibilities were vast and intriguing. I learned that they live in families and that there are more stories of interactions between Sasquatches and women and children because of the latter's gentleness and innocence, compared to the males of our species.

Taking that into consideration, I explored and began to become intimately familiar with all the details of the surrounding forests with my daughter Lilee in tow. Everything quickly became a game and an adventure. As the joy and excitement of her voice filled the air, I often thought that if there really was something out there watching and listening, it could not help but be drawn to her. We were daily amazed by the vast, intricate design of life in a rainforest. We would hike along game and old logging trails, climb massive fallen trees that became our pirate ships, and crawl within a maze of blackberry bushes to discover and become acquainted with as much as we possibly could.

While playing, Lilee and I would whoop, sing, and scream at the tops of our lungs and make all kinds of high-pitched noises. Even though we played pretend a lot, the reality of Bigfoot's existence in my daughter's mind has never been a fantasy. I know her acceptance of the cryptid now is solely based on belief, but I hope that her early exposure will make her desire to know more, and welcome new interactions and strange experiences with these mysterious creatures.

As we did these things, I took note when things were different from one day to the next. For example, branches broken high up in a specific pattern, small trees that appeared to have been pushed over to an exact angle on a path leading up a sharp uphill slope, and indentations in the mud and layers of leaves and moss that were of different sizes and were nearly always a substantial distance from one another. I say 'indentations' instead of footprints, because they did not all look like feet and cannot definitely be labeled as such. I found many clear tracks that I could confidently categorize as footprints, though, and some of the best ones would be in sequence on a path of indentations I had been following. With this in mind, I was never quick to assume that everything I saw was really a track.

On several later occasions when Joe and his crew became involved and I would point out a track line that had not been there the previous day and might have to do with activity noted on the previous night, Joe would often disregard it as nothing. Since he was the experienced one sharing his research techniques with me, I never openly disagreed with his opinions. However, there is one incident that I have pondered as fact or fiction more than any other that I believe is at least worth mentioning.

There was a day when I went out to check for tracks on my own. I was sure I would find some substantial evidence, considering the fresh snow from the day before and the distinct activity I had heard the previous night. To further explain, Rachel and I had been out on the deck late at night going through our normal routine of calls, listening, and waiting. We knew after only a short while that there was indeed at least one Bigfoot hanging out at the very edge of the woods on the far side of the yard on a nearly direct line from our current vantage point. We knew this not only because of the overbearing, penetrating presence it projected, but also because we heard repeated, clear rock knocks as well as very low grunts and faint, short whistles. The next sound came simultaneously from both sides of the yard. It seemed to be rustling because of weight shifting, in addition to the same faint, short whistles.

Rachel and I each stood on opposite sides of the deck as still as we physically and mentally could and strained to hear and interpret what could be going on out there because it was obvious that they were communicating with each other rather than responding to us. We never heard them come or go, even though the night was clear and quieter than usual. My opinion on this is that we were not being surrounded to satisfy their curiosity or to be threatened like prey. I think the most active and noisy creature located at the far end of our yard was possibly just letting however many more were out there know where we were and telling them not to make any unnecessary noises. I cannot, of course, even begin to try to fathom their reasoning or purpose, but I observed that the main creature was strongly authoritative and closer to us, while the others were more discreet, and that there was apparently no response to our efforts due to a pre-established agenda of their own. [I had never before and have not since heard the quiet whistling and deep grunts sounding like a distinct language that we heard that night.]

So, as I headed from the house toward the far end of the yard and the beginning of the forest, I replayed the events of the previous night in my head. After carefully surveying the immediate area, I noticed a hangover of branches heavy with wet snow making a cave over a hump of earth where the ground looked disturbed. I figured I would be able to just walk over and spot tracks in the snow, but the tree canopy had kept the snow from falling all the way to the ground in many areas, including this hill. By this time, I knew that authentic prints were nearly impossible to verify in the snow, because a path of tracks we humans make one day will melt down into larger tracks and look like signs of Bigfoot. There was just too much activity from people continually coming and going to reposition the cameras for me to remember where everyone had walked from one day to the next, even though I was the one who almost always went out with Joe and his crew to advise them on placement, switch memory cards, and help remember the many different locations of the cameras.

I would like to mention here how different I found both the activity and the overall feeling in the woods when it was just us, in contrast to when we had cameras and strangers there all the time. I am sure the

Squatches felt that their privacy had been invaded, and I think the trust they had in us was broken when we allowed this invasive research to take place. If I could go back and do it differently, I would, because I realize now how we could have discovered more had we taken more time to establish personal relationships, instead of just trying to attain "valid evidence."

I went into the cave on this small hill and saw how perfect the space was for something large to crouch down completely hidden and still view our house and balcony with no obstructions. I searched diligently for further clues. The only thing I found was a bunch of dead rubbish that had been pushed aside from a sort of door to the hideout. As I moved slowly over the terrain, I was constantly scanning the patches of snow for tracks, but a path through the snow never presented itself. In contrast, I realized that the unclear indentations on the floor and disturbances at or just above eye level I was noticing were all in places that avoided the snow. The more I searched and found ambiguous clues, the more perplexed I became.

The most concrete evidence I found included a huge entanglement of blackberry bushes that had been shoved aside to create a way to travel through; a cleared space within the bushes where a juvenile might have been put down to rest, but not big enough for anything bigger than myself; several hair samples — the largest amount I had collected at one time; and paths through narrow patches of small trees that had been forced apart to make room for something wider to pass through. I realize the possibility and still have to take into consideration the natural damage that occurs because of wind, wildlife, and various other natural phenomena.

The traces I was following were, as I mentioned, in areas away from the snow and in plain view of three cameras. I was exhilarated, thinking, "Yes! The proof we have all been hoping for." Pointing out what I considered the best of this evidence to Joe, I became embarrassed: he was unconvinced, especially since there was not a single picture of anything but me walking by on the cameras. Normally, I would just admit I'd been led astray by inexperience and imagination, but after taking more time to process all the details both from that night's experience and the tangible evidence I'd discovered, I remained convinced of my theory.

Although I was even more frustrated because I knew there was no real proof or explanation to validate my story, I can now be open to the possibility that Sasquatches could be and most likely are more than just animals. They may indeed possess abilities we do not know of or understand. I believe they definitely have far more acute senses than humans, which enables them to know not only who has been around, but also what a person's agenda is and whether it is threatening to them. Who really knows for certain, right?

Elizabeth's Visual Sighting

My eyes strained into the heavy, misty darkness, searching for something, anything. Every cell in my body seemed frozen in concentration, my heartbeat pounding through my body. The incredibly heavy fog that filled the air this night had made one of our forest friends braver than usual in its curiosity to approach our home. Rachel and I were outside on the balcony, which gave us the best vantage point to watch, listen, and attempt to imitate the various means of communication used by the subject of our newly discovered obsession. Its presence on this night was just as definite as on previous encounters I've had, but the sounds I clearly heard of crashing and stepping through the forest made us anticipate far more than just auditory responses. At this moment, I was thinking of everything I had personally witnessed that shed light on the existence and lifestyle of the mysterious creature, Bigfoot, yet I could only be fully convinced by seeing it with my own eyes. I felt as if I had put enough time, effort, and desire for truth into my search and studies to be worthy of this revelation. A real foot to go with the prints, a real arm covered in thick, silky hair to go with the hair samples, or just a body shape in the darkness would satisfy me.

I was gazing out into the fog with all this longing inside me for something real, and froze when the sounds of movement we had been following with a super intense spotlight stopped behind a tree about 30 feet away, and something looked directly at us with two dark, twinkling eyes. I saw the large, hairy outline of a round head with a diameter of 10-12 inches. A broad, flat nose started between the amber eyes and continued down to a slightly protruding mouth area. My first impression of the expression on its face was that it showed youthful curiosity. It stared at us three consecutive times from behind the tree in a matter of 40 seconds to a minute.

I knew what I was seeing was real and close and tangible enough to fill in the missing piece in my mind. Rachel and I savored every moment, paralyzed with awe. The creature then turned directly around and went up the hill and deeper into the empty darkness. It either seemed to be bored with playing hide-and-seek with us or satisfied that it had established visual contact and now wanted to rejoin its family or clan and maybe share its experience with them. We did not encounter or witness any further activity on this night. Our spotlight died on us after this, and Rachel and I stood there in utter amazement confirming with each other the details of what had just happened before running inside filled with adrenaline to share what we had seen.

Disclaimer: I would like to make it clear to readers at this time that I did not smell any bad odors or sense anything strong or strange like fearfulness, bad energy vibes, or any kind of imposed thoughts or feelings directed at my person when this encounter occurred. Because of this, I believe that lone creature did not feel threatened or intimidated by our persistent manner, but seemed to have allowed itself to be "caught" in direct view. I cannot explain why this particular one chose to reveal itself to us that night, when it could easily have stayed quietly hidden within the cover of the dark and fog to spy on us without us even realizing it was there. Even its noisy commotion before we saw it seemed intended to let us know it was there, much like a game. Perhaps there was a deeper purpose behind the intentional actions and behavior of this one being, but I guess we'll never know for sure.

The next morning we further confirmed the presence of a foreign creature — Bigfoot — around the very tree behind which we had spotted it. We asked Joe to come and investigate the area before anyone else, so the evidence would not be disturbed. What he found were several hair samples on the bark of the tree, fingerprints indented in the moss growing on a branch at 6½ or 7 feet from the ground, as well as potential footprints leading along several different paths, yet intertwined throughout the woods in the exact areas where we'd heard the sounds of movement. After hearing our description of the encounter as well as finding this evidence, Joe's only question was whether what we saw could possibly have been a raccoon up in the tree. Rachel and I seriously considered this for a moment, but then confidently asserted that it could not have been a raccoon or any other small animal because of the head shape and facial features we'd clearly seen. Despite Joe's ability to suggest a rational explanation for everything, he could not and did not try to dispute our story and took it as valid evidence.

In conclusion, how can our species have enough intelligence to be able to visually scan any given surface of the earth at any given time through satellite imaging or pictures taken by supersonic military aircraft, how can we travel to unbelievable depths of the ocean to discover and study completely new species of creatures, and yet have no knowledge of a massive mammal secretly living in a variety of habitats and climates all over the world? Furthermore, experiments are being conducted to perfect the science of genetically recreating and altering human DNA so that people can be cloned, and there is consistent yet subtle evidence pointing to the existence of extraterrestrial beings. So, why is it so hard to believe that there may be different planes of reality that humans are not always aware of, but are physically and spiritually affected by?

Most of us accept or at least consider the existence of unseen beings such as ghosts (haunted houses) and/or angels and demons (good vs. evil), yet we do not think that such beings could influence our perception of reality. I point all this out to show the mystery of everything out there in the universe and how it is all intertwined with our existence. What I do know is that we are just a minute part of it all. Because of these encounters I have shared with you, I will never look at a forest the same way again or stop searching for more adventures with Sasquatch. I believe every person needs to come to their own conclusions from their own life experience and perceptions, but I hope my own and my family's story will at least make you see that some legends can come true.

Rachel's Story

I breathed a sigh of relief as we finally pulled out onto the highway, heading towards yet another new home. Our family had moved frequently over the past several years, and we were becoming quite proficient at it. Dad was driving the moving truck filled with all of our earthly possessions. Mom, Elizabeth, Lilee, and the plants rode in our minivan, while I drove the pickup with our dogs as my only company.

As we meandered south and then west through the changing Washington landscape, I thought about what the future might hold for us. I had resided in, traveled throughout, and camped all over Montana, Idaho, Washington, and Alaska for the past six years, but I knew that coastal living was going to be very different for my family and me. We were taking a serious risk with this move. We had seen the house we were about to call home only in pictures on the computer screen. None of us had ever visited the area before or knew a single soul who lived there. The house we found was fairly expensive and would require all four of us adults to work. I only hoped that Elizabeth and I could find jobs.

My excitement grew as I caught sight of Mt. Rainier and began to smell saltwater in the air. I recalled the times in my life that I had spent near the ocean. I thought that this move would be a really nice change, that maybe this time we would establish ourselves somewhere and put down some roots. I sat back and settled in for the rest of the long drive.

The New House

As we neared the coast, the sky darkened and heavy clouds charged in from almost every direction. The heavens opened and poured out on us. I could hardly see through my windshield, and we were bumper to bumper trying to maneuver our way through Tacoma. I knew it rained a lot over here, but I just hoped that it wouldn't always be this bad.

As we kept truckin', the rain slowed but it was still steadily falling. I knew we were only a few minutes away from our destination, so I pulled off to get a good look around. People were driving awfully fast down the narrow, winding two-lane highway, despite these conditions. My eyes kept scanning, and I saw many small, skinny, tall houses crammed between the road and the water. Wow. That's really living on the edge.

Everything was lush and green. The trees were thick everywhere that there wasn't a road or a building. I hurried back onto the highway, almost speeding in my anticipation to see our new house. A few more turns, curves, and hills and I pulled into the driveway of what was now our home. It was large and green, nearly camouflaged against the towering spruce, fir, and cedars surrounding the property. As I turned off the engine and climbed out of the truck, the smell of salty rainforest assaulted my senses. It was sprinkling softly, causing the woods to whisper in the gentle shower. It was a world away from the dry and rocky north Columbia River country that we had left only a day earlier. I shivered slightly as a breeze blew through every layer of clothing I wore. I steeled myself as I walked up the stairs toward my future, or what would quickly become the most paranormal, strange, yet intensely awesome experience of my life so far.

Even from the very first days on the coast, something seemed odd. Out of place. All right, it was downright spooky at times. I remember waking up one morning, and mom telling me how the night before dad had heard very loud stomping in the woods and the sounds of a very large object being hurled. There were strange moaning, hooting, and screaming sounds at night. I was not used to this kind of forest. It was dark and wet, always dripping, muddy. It distorted sounds and voices, muffling them at times. Still, there were occasions when a noise came from what you could swear was right around the next tree, yet you'd find out it was actually many, many yards and trees away. It was like a sound vortex that twisted and warped noises. Creepy.

My mother has already described to you the events that took place on November 22, the day she and I heard the very loud, distinct call coming from nearby in the trees. It was a sound similar to, yet completely unlike, anything I'd heard before in my life. It kind of sounded like a wild banshee with a frog in its throat. There was a four to five second scream followed by a few deep, guttural grunts. I had heard a cougar before, and it definitely wasn't that, not to mention that there weren't cougars in this area. A wolf? No way. What kind of a wolf grunts and screams? Perhaps an elk, but since when are my dogs so scared of an elk that they come running back terrified? The volume, depth, length, and deeply emotional quality of this voice ruled out, at least in our minds, any scientifically classified North American mammal, bird, insect, or other creature. The lung capacity alone required to make such a sound was far more than any human or animal is capable of, as far as I know.

This left me with few options. I tentatively came to the conclusion that there must be a creature or even forest people of sorts that had managed to stay hidden from humans, coming out only when they wanted to be seen or heard. Pictures of the abominable snowman and Harry and the Hendersons passed through my mind. I quickly dismissed those fairy tales, as daily this myth began to materialize in front of my eyes. This legend became a reality, a shadow that lingered close, teasing me with its presence yet never completely revealing itself. Still, what did anybody really know about Bigfoot? We all needed some answers.

My life changed one day when a legend became real. A myth became a shadow that visited our home. Strange moaning, howling, hooting, and crying filled the night air. Every day became an adventure, as I learned more about these amazing creatures that we lived among. This is an account of some of my encounters with Sasquatch.

Although my mother has described (in great detail) our experiences with Bigfoot, she has asked me to add a little from my own perspective. One of the most amazing things to me is how many different sounds the

Sasquatch uses to communicate. Not only are there dozens of vocal patterns and calls, they also use wood knocking or rock knocking to locate one another. I decided that I wanted to locate one for myself. What I didn't expect was to be answered. Continually. For hours at a time. On several different occasions.

I have been interested in and have studied wildlife, forestry, conservation, ecology, natural resources, and so on, for almost my whole life. I remember being seven years old and having a subscription to *Ranger Rick Magazine*. I wanted to be Ranger Rick someday. Actually, I am still occasionally referred to as such. I also had a very old CD-ROM game all about Yellowstone National Park. Where did my mom find things that were so fun yet educational at the same time?

I enjoy nothing more than sitting by a burbling creek, with the boughs of birch and cedar swaying and dancing all around me and the sound of birds chirping and deer rummaging in the brush near my resting spot. I love the way the forest floor is covered with pine needles, the way they crunch and crackle when you walk on them, and the way they smell at the end of a hot, dry summer. I love watching a moose cow and her calf through my binoculars as they twist and climb their way up a steep embankment. I love the smell of fish and seeing a thousand seagulls circle and then perch atop the waves to see what scraps they can find. I guess what I'm trying to say is that I feel most at home among nature. It's soothing to me and I have always had a deep desire to study it and understand how it works. It can't be very hard, then, to imagine how excited I was to have a whole new ecosystem to discover and study. Of course, my subject of study quickly changed, and I was overjoyed when a field investigator, Joe, entered the story. He helped to answer our many questions, and taught us to see our situation in a whole new light.

Joe brought motion-sensing cameras. He brought night vision infrared goggles. He brought crews of experienced researchers, trackers, and investigators. And he brought answers. He assured us of our sanity and told us countless stories just like ours. He took us on hikes while pointing out little details in the "woodwork" of the forest. Just tiny things that I would never have noticed or seen the meaning of, but to him it meant there had been a disturbance of some sort. He showed us game trails, tracks, hair, and even scat. I learned how sound travels through the forest and how to distinguish its direction. I saw large branches that had been twisted and snapped liked toothpicks, and whole areas of brush flattened like a pancake. Joe told us about the many expeditions he had been on in search of these elusive giants. He had been an avid hunter all his life and had spent many years in the deep wilderness areas of America. I knew I could trust his knowledge, experience, and instincts in the forest.

Joe, Barb, and the others taught me that there are many different factors that researchers must consider. You cannot just look at a thing from one side: you must explore it from every angle to get a complete picture. Meaning, one person's story of an encounter could vary a great deal from another's. Knowledge is power, and the more I learned, the more prepared and curious I felt. I began to experiment as my comprehension and awareness grew. I attempted to imitate the sounds and behavior of my forest friends, vigorously trying to establish some sort of communication. I felt silly and awkward at first, until I started getting responses. Every day became an adventure as I learned more about these amazing creatures. I would now like to share with you some of my personal experiences and encounters with Sasquatch.

Rock Knocking

Almost every evening, my sister and I would sit on our balcony to become familiar with the sounds of the forest. We would imitate the noises we heard, as well as clapping, singing, common Bigfoot calls… anything we could think of to get a response. One night, I took a rock the size of my hand and struck it twice on the wooden railing of the balcony. About thirty seconds later, from somewhere in the vast blackness of the woods, came the response we were looking for. We heard what sounded like two rocks larger than mine in size being struck or knocked together. A few minutes later I tried it again, and again I was answered. I knocked four times, and then he would knock four times. This continued for a couple of hours. I called Joe, who promptly came over, despite the lateness of the hour. He sat quietly and listened to our noisy exchange. He had never heard anything like it, he said. We didn't always get an answer. At one point, all responses ceased for over an hour. We thought the beast had gotten bored and moved on, but then the knocking started again, this time from a completely different direction and distance.

There were other occasions during the day as well as at night when I could hear this knocking. But never again was I answered so continuously for such a length of time, and to the point where they were almost imitating the number and rhythm of my knocks.

I Hit a Wall

Our backyard was a small grassy area surrounded on three sides by trees and on one side by our house. The night was bright from the moon and there was an eerie feeling, as if they were close by. Elizabeth and I went to make our presence known. We danced and sang about the field, whooping and hollering and hoping to see or hear something. On one side of the field was a steep, wooded hill where we often heard footsteps and branches cracking. We knew it could be deer, coyote, or even the giant wolf that lived in the area. We continued on with our display, all the while still feeling a presence. As I walked toward the far end of the field, something happened that I can only describe as "hitting a wall." It was nothing physical, as I was standing in an open area. I cannot explain it, but I knew there was a Sasquatch very close, possibly on the edge of the lawn behind a large tree. He sent me a clear mental message saying, "Just to let you know, I am here. Don't come any closer." I was walking and something made me jump back midstride, with a definite warning to stay away. It was not a fearful or threatening feeling at all. It only confirmed more fully in my mind that there really is something out there that wants to stay hidden from the world. For now.

I saw nothing with my eyes and heard nothing with my ears, but it was an experience as real as you and me. It scared me and excited me all at once. I'll not soon forget it.

Face in the Fog

There is a part in all of us that won't believe something until we see it with our own two eyes. Regardless of finding countless tracks and hair samples on our property and hearing all sorts of strange sounds, I couldn't totally accept the existence of a creature I'd never seen. Until one night.

The fog was thick. The wind was howling through the trees. The atmosphere was heavy with long-hidden secrets. There were loud crashing noises coming from the forest very close to our home. The entire household was still with excitement and anticipation. Elizabeth and I crouched on the balcony. We held our breath while frantically following the sound of breaking branches with our fast-dying spotlight. The noise went left, then back up the hill. Then to the right. Back and forth we searched. It came closer. Then the noise stopped. Our light was but a dim yellow glow, yet we looked hard in the direction where we'd last heard the crashing. The trees and the brush were very thick.

"Wait!" I whispered. "Go back!"

I had seen a faint glimmer or a shadow. Or a very small movement. The visibility was so poor and the fog was so heavy that it was difficult to know exactly what it was that I had seen.

"Look!" Elizabeth gasped as she focused the spotlight in one place.

My eyes searched desperately where the light shone. It barely illuminated a large tree about thirty feet from where we were. There was a thick branch that protruded from the trunk almost horizontally, then curved upwards. This branch was six or seven feet from the ground. From above the branch, peering out from behind the massive trunk was a pair of large, round, amber eyes. Surrounding those eyes was the dark, misty outline of a fuzzy head with barely discernable facial features. They were human-like but larger, with a flatter nose and large lips. The eyes were deep-set, with the top of the head several inches above the brow. It lasted but a few breathless seconds, and then he was gone. We continued to look, but our light died shortly after that. We stayed outside for a long time that night just listening to the stomping around our backyard.

Early the next morning, we called Joe to come over and examine the area. What he found blew us all away. He checked first by the tree where we'd seen it. The ground around the base and roots was very disturbed. The branch that I previously described was covered with a thick, soft, spongy moss. There was an impression on the top side of the branch, like that of an arm resting on it. Joe also found one or two long black hairs in the moss. We stood on the balcony in daylight as he measured where we'd seen the face. It was approximately eight feet above the ground. Joe also found footprints all over our property, as well as many freshly broken branches.

There are many more layers to this encounter that I have not gone into detail about. We believe there was more than one creature so close that night. Perhaps they felt more comfortable and safe due to the fog and wind. One large male walked into the open field right in front of a motion-sensor camera. The image we received was blurry at best, but there was a definite outline of teeth, a shoulder, an arm, abs, and an upper leg.

The Chase

One rainy Sunday afternoon, only a few weeks before we moved away, Elizabeth and I were practicing our choir music for that day's rehearsal. By that point in time, we were quite used to the sensation of a Sasquatch presence. Molly alerted us as she ran barking up and then back down the wooded hill outside our window. We looked at each other and knew we had a visitor. Mom came into the room a minute later, also to point out the presence we had all felt approach our home only a few moments before.

Elizabeth and I had a couple of hours until choir practice, so we slipped on our mud boots and quickly hiked up the hill towards where we heard and felt the creature. Molly ran ahead jumping back and forth, obviously hot on the trail of something. We kept jogging along through the forest, looking for any imprints in the mud, broken branches, or even a foul smell left by a recent occupant of the area. We continued on deeper and deeper into the woods that were crisscrossed with hundreds of trails and logging roads. We began cutting our own trail through the thick, soggy brush, and soon felt that our little visitor had led us on a wild goose chase and then made a quick, easy getaway and left us behind. I had never been this far into the mysterious abyss of these woods, and we decided to keep going to see what we could find in this place where people rarely came. On and on we hiked, hoping to see something familiar to assure us we were at least getting closer to home. We saw many impressions in the earth, as well as huge areas that had been pushed back effortlessly and flattened. We saw branches snapped right off the trunks of trees eight to twelve feet high. It was eerie, and I did not like the feeling of being lost in such a strange place. It was like walking through a stranger's home, yet who and where the inhabitants were I only wished I knew. Needless to say, we returned home soaking wet, muddy, and very late for practice.

I've added this to point out how badly we wanted to see this thing. To really get a good look: of course, preferably in daylight, but also preferably not too close up. Yet it really was like being teased and taunted. Those creatures knew we were there before we knew anything about them. Almost daily they let us know of their close proximity, yet they chose to remain concealed. I merely hope for the day when the cloak that covers the truth about Sasquatch will be removed and we will come to truly understand them.

Paranormal or What?

I wasn't going to add this part of my story, but my mom convinced me that it was significant. It is perhaps the most unexplainable of all my encounters. I almost feel silly telling about it. I have no answers, only questions, about what happened. Maybe someday I'll understand.

I was awakened in the middle of the night. I listened intently and my heart pounded in my chest. I had heard something. The first thing I thought of was Bigfoot. His presence was strong. There it was again. Someone was in the hallway outside of my bedroom. The floor was especially squeaky in that one spot. Odd. It was 3:30 AM. Who could be up at this hour? And what exactly was it that had awakened me from a deep sleep so suddenly? My sister's bedroom was on one side of mine and my niece's bedroom was on the other. My dog, who was usually the first one to alert me of anyone's presence, was strangely silent.

I waited a few minutes, then decided to go look. I opened my door and peered down the hallway towards the kitchen and living room. There was a small light on above the stove, but other than that, it was quite dark. I listened for a second, but continued on when I heard nothing. I walked to the dining room, where there were several large windows and glass doors. I had the strangest feeling that if I looked out the windows, I would see a face. Suddenly, I became very scared. I went back to bed, still wondering about what I heard.

The next day I talked to all of the family who had been at home the night before. I thought perhaps somebody had had trouble sleeping and was up in the middle of the night roaming the house in the dark. But no, nobody had been up at that hour.

Like I said, I have no explanation. But I do know what I heard. Perhaps a Sasquatch really did come into my house, walked down my hallway, went back outside, and then stood there watching me. I also believe it could have just been a spirit. Maybe it was nothing. Maybe I'll never know.

A Closing Note

In all my years studying both animals of the wild and people of the wilder, I've never known a being like Sasquatch. Their intelligence seems to exceed ours at times, and yet they are only beasts. They are very family-oriented and seem to live in groups, yet they have an incredible way of staying hidden. There is overwhelming evidence and many reports of their existence, yet their elusiveness despite their massive size is unheard of in the world of science today. We are more willing to believe in dinosaurs and aliens than in a very shy primate type of creature living in our own mountains.

My mind came alive, and I began to actively study anything and everything documented about the famous Bigfoot. It became a hobby (or perhaps an obsession) for my family. While our friends and relatives laughed at us, we ourselves could hardly believe what we were experiencing. It has awakened in me a desire to continue my studies on wildlife, with a special interest in cryptozoology (the study of hidden animals).

No matter where I live, I will always find a patch of quiet woods to visit. I will stand, and at the top of my lungs I will whoop and whistle and holler, hoping just maybe to come into contact with my forest friends again. It is true what they say, "You don't find them. They find you." And I'm so glad they did!

5. Research

As we continued our research or quest for information, we were and still are amazed at just how little is really known about Bigfoot. There are, however, certain circumstances and patterns that have been recorded, and we will seek to present these. Some of you will no doubt find much of this information somewhat commonplace and dry reading if you have previously studied Bigfoot, but we don't want to take what you may or may not already know for granted. Therefore, it was our goal to create lists that are as thorough as possible.

Names of Bigfoot

Let's start with the many names that Bigfoot is called. Early on, they were usually called "Wild Hairy Man," but since 1957 when some loggers found many big footprints in one area, they have been named Bigfoot. Below are some other names used around the world.

North American Ape, Sasquatch, Squatch, Yowie, Abominable Snowman, Wildman, Skunk Ape, Skookum, Swamp Monkey, Forest People, Man of the Woods, Stick Indians, Night People, Wood Man, Bush Man, Orang Pendek, Wookie.

In addition to these, there are literally dozens of other names, each one coming from a different Indian tribe, such as:

The Big Man, Swamp Monster, Elder Brother, Hairy Man, Wood Devil, Brush Ape, Night Screamer, Dog Man, Goat Man, Swamp Devil, and many more.

Reports

Certainly as the population increases in rural areas, Bigfoot encounters will increase, and, hopefully, so will documented reports. Unfortunately, I have read that for every one sighting that is reported there may be 10 to 15 that are not. Obviously, most people are embarrassed, frightened, in denial, or do not want to be mocked or laughed at, which is not uncommon. These days, most reports are either called in or emailed in to the various Bigfoot websites that seem to be continually popping up all over the internet. People that saw a hairy creature cross the road in front of their car back in 1964 are just now sharing their experiences because:

#1. There is someplace and someone to actually tell their story to now that will most likely find them credible and not laugh at them, and

#2. They can tell the story and remain completely anonymous if they choose to do so.

Most sightings that are reported on these websites are reports of a creature crossing the road in front of someone's car, or perhaps they've heard screams or noises or smelled strange, nasty odors while out camping or hiking, or something of the sort. Although these kinds of reports are good and give general info about a Bigfoot — approximate weight, size, color, or even perhaps facial features — this information does not really tell us who or what a Bigfoot really is, where they come from, how they live, what their family or clan structure is, how long they live, or even what they eat.

We believe that this type of information must come from long-term personal study and ongoing relationships with the Bigfoot. Even in our own experiences, we feel we have only seen hints of unknown possibilities.

Again — and there is so much guessing at this point, but why not hazard a guess — and I say this from a woman's point of view: perhaps the approach with these creatures should be like the approach that a man might have toward a woman. (I can see the rolling eyes of some male readers now…stay with me please). If he gets to know her just by the "facts" of who she is, height, weight, hair color, or even a photo, these are still only FACTS! This gives him enough info to brag to his friends about all he knows, BUT he really doesn't know the woman yet. He doesn't know her personality, her likes and dislikes. He's not showing any respect or love for her. He just trying to get something from her for his own gain. Trust me, she's not stupid and it won't be long before she says, "Hit the road, Jack, and don't you come back no more!" The point is, the Bigfoot seem to be very sensitive creatures that are able to discriminate heartfelt interest from grasping curiosity.

This may sound ridiculous or like emotional nonsense, but something MAJOR is lacking in Bigfoot research today, despite the fact that some are trying to be as "scientific" as possible. It's like a person who memorizes the Bible so they can recite passages and impress others around them. Unfortunately, most people who do this really don't know the TRUE Jesus or the Love of God, they only have words or knowledge in their heads. There's a huge difference between legalism and grace with love.

Considering the major increase in transportation, communications, and technology, particularly in surveillance-type equipment, you would think that tracking Bigfoot and at least getting some good pictures would be simple. Not so. In fact, our personal experience has proved that the more cameras we set out, the less Bigfoot activity. We have heard that this is a common occurrence. Ours were camouflaged game-trail cameras set with infrared and motion detectors that were placed in hidden areas. One day, there would be footprints along a game trail, so we would reposition the cameras there. The next day footprints would show up through the bushes next to the trail, obviously to avoid the cameras.

When speculating on this, one can only guess why it is so. Perhaps they can smell the plastic or whatever material the camera is made of. Maybe they can hear very subtle sounds that we cannot hear emitted by the camera. Maybe the "eye" of the camera resembles the end of a pistol or rifle. Maybe they see into the infrared. Maybe they sense the intention of the researchers, and hence take other paths that seem safer. Who knows?

Family Units

They seem to live in family units, possibly with one dominant male, several females, and then the babies and juveniles. Many think that it is the latter who are the bolder, less concealed ones and sometimes seem to enjoy playing "I dare you!" with high-speed oncoming cars. Perhaps it is an initiation into adulthood.

No one knows for sure, but there is a recent belief that Bigfoot live in clans with a dominant male, probably the biggest and strongest one, along with other males, females, juveniles (the young Bigfoot), and infants. Clans may range from approximately eight to 20 creatures, each having its own job. Several gather food, while others are like soldiers guarding the area, and so on. I spoke to a man who believed that different clans came together at different times of the year.

It seems that there are different types or species of Bigfoot all around the earth. They seem to look different in different geographical areas. For instance, the Skunk Ape, which is found in Florida and southern USA, has long hair and perhaps fangs, while other species have straight teeth (no fangs), shorter hair, rounder heads or more cone-like heads, or even flat heads. We have even heard that there may be some male rogue Bigfoot. Like people, I imagine each one has a different personality.

What They Eat

Bigfoot are most likely omnivores. Berries, roots, bark, leaves, and other items seem to be just as necessary as deer, elk, bobcats, rodents, frogs, rabbits, even chickens from your coop, or garbage from the local dumpster. Can you imagine the daily caloric intake of something that weighs 300-900+ pounds? Witnesses have seen Bigfoot creatures walking off with a calf under their arms. I think they probably eat a wider variety of foods than we know, but I don't think they would eat any of us, at least we hope not. What do they eat? Anything they want to.

Nocturnal

Bigfoot seem to be mostly nocturnal creatures, but of course, they have been seen and heard during daylight hours, as well. They obviously can stay hidden better at night, and it seems that most Bigfoot want to stay hidden from humans. Perhaps they understand the power, greed, and danger of most human beings. We've heard that some types of Bigfoot seem to be very curious and somewhat friendly with humans, while others do everything they can to stay away from us.

In our experience, we've heard them both during the day and the night, but their presence has always been stronger and more active after dark.

Where They Live

It used to be a myth that Bigfoot were only found in the Pacific Northwest or western Canada. We now know that sightings have been reported from every state in the USA, including Wahiawa, Hawaii, where they are called Aikanaka — the giant of the pineapple fields. One witness, a visitor to the area, reports clearly seeing an approximately eight-foot-tall male and a seven-foot-tall female in the area. Locals also report such sightings. Reports have also come from and continue to come in from all over the world, including Australia, China, Europe, the Pacific Islands, and South America. The Bigfoot are thought to have regular migration patterns. This has become one of the latest areas of field research.

We recently came across some riveting information that there are Bigfoot creatures, no less than a thousand of them, living in a certain area of the Solomon Islands in the South Pacific. Not only have such legends been passed down through the generations, but the locals of Guadalcanal tell stories about the creatures to any listening ear, as well as to "outsiders" who carry their tales abroad. The descriptions fit our North American Bigfoot almost exactly, only they seem to be taller in most cases. There are even reports of people that are called half-castes or quarter-castes and are the result of humans breeding with these creatures. They live in villages on the island. If this is true, we would immediately come to the conclusion that they are not primates of any sort, because primates and humans cannot reproduce with each other. We hope others will follow up on this information and go on expeditions to determine the truth of these tales.

There are also reports that some of these creatures are VERY big, like at least 20 feet tall, are cannibals, and are often a threat to locals who might wander into their living areas.

They have been known to live in caves, water drains, tunnels, and of course, in shelters in the forests that they build themselves with tree and bush branches. People have stumbled upon dug-out areas in the ground with tree limbs covering them. The shelter structure we saw in the meadow up the hill from our house had a dug-out area that looked like a nest. Perhaps it was a work in progress because it wasn't big enough for a Bigfoot yet, but it was about four feet deep, four feet long, and three feet wide.

The Smell

Bigfoot sightings are often, but not always, accompanied by a putrid smell that has sometimes been described as musty, swampy, or like skunk, garbage, wet dog, urine, feces, sewer, or a combination of several of these smells mixed together. The odor can be strong enough to make your eyes burn.

Now, I never actually smelled anything bad around our house, but my husband Wayne did smell that skunk smell at least three times, while the girls smelled a very musty, dirty smell as a Bigfoot grunted and ran up the hill away from where they were standing.

On the other hand, sometimes there is no smell whatsoever. There is a species of gorilla that actually has glands under its armpits that can release at will a horrible smell to ward off its enemies. Perhaps Bigfoot has similar glands. No one knows for sure… yet.

Footprints

Footprints have now been collected by the thousands in the form of plaster casts, and are probably one of the strongest proofs of the existence of Bigfoot. Not so many years ago, dermal ridges were discovered on some of these castings. Dermal ridges are like the palm lines on our hands. No two prints are the same. Good footprints will also sometimes show a line running horizontally in the middle of the foot, suggesting that the foot can flex in the middle, something a human foot cannot do.

One print that we found and measured was 16" long by 7" wide, as you can see in the picture. People have found and recorded prints up to 20" long. Another important thing when measuring prints that we learned much later is to remember to also measure the depth of the print; how far down the print has sunk into the dirt, mud, snow, or whatever.

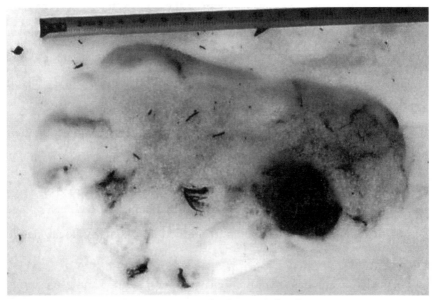

Figure 13: Sixteen-inch by seven-inch track in the snow.

Bigfoot in History

"Big, Hairy Wildmen" or "Hairy Forest People" descriptions are found in early historical reports. In 986 A.D., Leif Erickson wrote in his voyage journal about monsters in the New World that were very large, hairy, and had black eyes.

Zana was a female Abnauayu, which is what a Bigfoot-type creature in the Western Caucasus Mountains of Russia is called. She was apparently caught and kept caged for several years until she was tame. She had two sons and two daughters, the fathers being human. The first two babies died after she washed them in the cold waters of a river right after giving birth. She died in the 1880s or 1890s. Her body was never discovered in its grave, but the body of her second son was, not so long ago around 1978. You can read the lengthy and incredible story yourself at http://www.bigfootencounters.com/articles/zana.htm.

Lewis and Clark claimed to have seen similar creatures in their explorations, as described in their diaries. In the book *Letters of the Lewis and Clark Expedition, with Related Documents, 1783-1854* by Donald Jackson, there are stories of Little People as well as savage beasts or mountain devils, some recounted to them by local native tribesmen.

In 1807, Canadian explorer and trapper David Thompson wrote about a series of footprints that as a seasoned woodsman he'd never seen before. The prints were 14" long by 8" wide, with four toes, each toe being 4" long. The print was sunk down 6" deep in the snow.

In 1840, Reverend Elkanah Walker, a Protestant missionary, recorded stories of giants among the Native Americans living in Spokane, Washington.

Another interesting and somewhat bizarre story comes from Canada back in 1924. A man named Albert Ostman was camping way out in the wilderness, where he claims he was picked up by a Bigfoot in his sleeping bag one night and kept for six days until he managed to escape. The story is quite long and you may enjoy hearing it in his own words, so here are two links for that purpose: www.youtube.com/watch?v=E8arvOrUV6E or www.bfro.net/GDB/show_report.asp?id=1091. Ostman has been interviewed many times over a period of decades and his story seems to remain consistent.

In Robert Morgan's book about Daniel Boone, it states that while living in the wilderness, Boone encountered great hairy monsters similar to the "yahoos" in *Gulliver's Travels*. A "yahoo'" is a legendary humanoid creature described as vile, savage, filthy, and having unpleasant habits.

In a book by John Mack Faragher, *Daniel Boone: The Life and the Legend of an American Pioneer*, the author states that Boone claims to have killed a ten foot "monster."

By far, the Native American communities are perhaps our greatest source of information about Sasquatch throughout the generations. Their stories are passed down to children and grandchildren. Many ancient Indian tribes, such as the Kwakiutl Indians in British Columbia, even carved man-beast faces on their totem poles.

David Paulides has written two great books on the Sasquatch-Native American connection, one called *The Hoopa Project*, and his most recent one, *Tribal Bigfoot*. The drawings were done by a forensic artist after David interviewed many natives and non-natives who had personal and sometimes up-close encounters with Bigfoot.

Kathy Strain also has written a book called, *Giants Cannibals & Monsters: Bigfoot in Native Culture*, which includes over 150 stories of folklore from Native American tribes. Henry Franzoni, a longtime researcher, has an interesting read called *In the Spirit of Seatco*.

One Native American I talked with had several tales. Apparently, it was a well-known fact that the Sasquatch lived in the forest near a particular bay. The muskeg (bogland) was soft and squishy there. Many places in the forest held strange sights: trees that had been pulled up by their roots, turned over, and stuck back in the muskeg. The locals believed the Bigfoot were doing that to mark their territories.

Two miners came to the area, hiking through the forest up to an area of large cliffs. They'd apparently found a large gold vein, and of course were very excited about it. They stayed in a nearby cabin, but had some nighttime visitors that threw rocks at the cabin all night. The next day, the miners spotted large trees with branches broken and twisted high up over their heads. This story ends with the miners being purportedly chased through the forest by the creatures all the way down to the water's edge. Despite the gold find, the miners claimed they would never return to the area.

To read some more fascinating and strange stories, get Thom Powell's book, my favorite, *The Locals: A Contemporary Investigation of the Bigfoot Phenomenon.*

The stories go on and on. It makes for a great internet search!

The Body Search

The question most often asked is "How come no one has ever found a body?"

The answer is probably that, like other creatures that die in the deep forests, the carcass is eaten and disassembled by various critters that are the "cleanup crew."

Or, if they are really intelligent creatures and as human-like as some think they are, they perhaps actually bury their own. There are now a small number of witnesses who have recently spoken out, claiming they have actually seen the creatures bury their own dead. There have been some reports of finding Bigfoot "graveyards." On the other hand, others say that perhaps bodies have been found, but the local and federal governments have stepped in and are keeping it all hush-hush. It's possible. Governments don't want to have to deal with mass hysteria and demands to send in SWAT teams of hunters to kill off those dangerous monsters in the woods for the sake of public safety.

At this point, it's all theory.

Why Don't More People See Them?

I suppose it's rather difficult to wrap your mind around the thought that a six- to nine-foot creature weighing 300 to 900 pounds or more can be so shy and so elusive, but that seems to be exactly the case. However, there are thousands upon thousands of sightings and encounters being reported like never before, thanks to the internet and Bigfoot websites.

Maybe they are just so intelligent that they know their plight once a human being gets ahold of them: captured, caged, examined, photographed, tested, dissected, injected, isolated, and put on display for worldwide viewing.

Besides, the majority of the population lives in larger towns or cities where Bigfoot rarely visit. They're smarter than that.

Where Are the Pictures?

Since there are probably more investigators and researchers in the field now than ever before, with all of their low-tech and high-tech equipment, including motion-sensor infrared cameras behind every tree (well, almost), how come there are so few pictures? How come when the cameras were set out around our yard, the Bigfoot, who we knew were definitely there, avoided them?

I don't believe they "know" what a camera is actually for, but is it so strange to think that they can actually see the infrared from the camera?

I also believe, based on conversations I've had with other witnesses, that there are pictures out there taken by these witnesses, but folks are keeping silent about it. They are avoiding the circus and the hype of the media to protect themselves, their relations, and the Bigfoot.

Unfortunately, some people are heavily influenced by what's on the TV set, which may be running constantly in many homes. This often adds to the belief that if something, anything, isn't being presented publicly through the news on the tube, it can't, after all, be true. Besides, if a picture was shown to the public, there would still be plenty of people demanding more proof. "Show me a body" would be the next step. Hasn't that already happened plenty of times? The Patterson-Gimlin film of the 1960s is a perfect example of this. I think as humans we have an unquenchable thirst for knowledge and information.

Children

Bigfoot seems to be especially attracted to children and the sounds they make.

We can personally attest to that. Our granddaughter Lilee has a very joyous, outgoing personality with a kind, hearty laugh that usually gets others laughing also. She's an active, high-energy four-year-old who loves to be outdoors. While we lived on the coast, she would hang out in the forest next to the house where a tire swing was strung high up in the trees. I'm sure her shrieks of delight were heard by anything or anyone within a half-mile distance.

When she learned about Bigfoot, one of her favorite hobbies, which she still does to this day, is calling for the big guys, "Whoop, whoop," which she yells loudly in a high-pitched voice. It is so adorable, but of course I'm the gramma, so I would say that.

Her daily reports as she comes running breathless and wide-eyed into the house are, "We've got a track! Come see!" It could be any kind of track, but at least she's looking.

She even told a little neighbor girl down the block, who became her friend, about Bigfoot. Lilee taught her how to "whoop, whoop," and they would be up in the woods together (supervised, of course) whooping... much to the chagrin of her mother.

So we started calling Lilee our "Bigfoot bait," because we highly suspected that Bigfoot might be attracted to kids, even before we had read other incidents of Bigfoot encounters involving kids.

Sure enough, the stories continue to pour in that Bigfoot have been seen in the yards of homes, playgrounds, recreational areas, and at the bedroom windows of children. I have never read or heard of any harmful incidents. This could be a reasonable clue that Bigfoot are basically gentle and harmless, coupled with the fact that they have numerous chances to hurt or kill humans, but do not.

Since they seem to deeply care for and are highly protective of their own young, perhaps this is another reason for their attraction to human children. Stories are documented that they may actually seek playmates for their young. There are people who say they have played with Bigfoot juveniles when they were younger. As a matter of fact, we know of a man, a friend of a friend sort of thing, who told me some very interesting stories. He is from Alaska and a Native American, a chief and last in the line of his family. When he was barely four years old, he was at his grandfather's summerhouse in a fishing village near a bay. He was standing on the back porch, when an approximately eight-foot-tall, grayish male Sasquatch came out of the forest and walked directly up to him. As a young boy, he was not afraid, but began giggling. He lifted up his hand to the face of this sweet, pungent-smelling creature, which took his hand and forearm, drawing it to his own face, and he began stroking its hair. He noticed six fingers on each hand, then looking down, he also saw six toes on each foot. The man says it was as if it happened yesterday, not decades ago, and that the hair on the Sasquatch felt "silky."

Meanwhile, when the mother, who was inside the house, heard her son giggling, she came to the door. Seeing this large creature with her son, she screamed and yelled for the grandfather. He came to the door and said, "Oh, don't worry. He won't hurt him." The joke is that the grandfather was saying that the little boy would not hurt the huge Sasquatch, not the other way around. The creature turned and walked back into the trees, leaving the young boy crying on the porch. The man said the creature was very much a mixture of man and ape. When I asked him where he thought the Sasquatch came from, his answer made me chuckle. He said," I don't know and it doesn't matter. We don't have to know everything."

I am not naïve about such encounters: Bigfoot are big, very big, and very strong, and just like humans, some Bigfoot surely may be dangerous killers. Many Native American tribes, as well as other cultures around the world, have stories that the "Wild Men" or "Forest People" come out of the woods and steal children because they are cannibals. These tales are to be respected and not taken lightly.

Communication

Verbal

Bigfoot seem to have several ways of communicating with each other. Their purported vocalizations or sounds can be found at several websites on the internet. Some common sounds are whoops, whistles, grunts, growls, howls, screams, monkey-type chatter, and clapping sounds that resemble rocks or sticks being knocked together. Recent recordings seem to have even uncovered a type of language that they are speaking to one another. In Bigfoot circles it is called a "Samurai" language, and sounds as if it could be a mixture of some Asian/Oriental dialect and Native American language.

I have even heard one witness say he believes that *some* Bigfoot are actually speaking English, but are speaking so quickly that the words are simply running together. (Perhaps if we slow down some of the recordings of purported Sasquatch-talk and play them backwards, we might even hear "Paul is dead!" like the Beatles' hoax many decades ago.

Scott Nelson, a crypto-linguist of thirty-plus years for the US Navy, is presently doing in-depth research on Bigfoot language. He has logged thousands of hours of transcription. He is currently teaching Russian, Spanish, Persian, philosophy, and comparative religion at Wentworth College in Missouri. He states, "We have verified that these creatures use language, by the human definition of it. With the recognition and acceptance that these creatures do indeed speak and understand a complex language, a greater effort will be made to collect voice recordings and our analysis of the language will improve. Now that we have a precedent and techniques established for this study, this process will certainly become easier."

As of June 2010, Mr. Nelson has devised the first-ever Bigfoot alphabet. It is called SPA, the Sasquatch Phonetic Alphabet. It was developed for those in Bigfoot research (that would be *anyone* out in the woods attempting to befriend these creatures), helping them to communicate with common sounds that Bigfoot are known to make. It is a groundbreaking effort!

Bigfoot have also been known to mimic sounds in the forest, from birds to campers snoring! We've heard one mimic an ambulance siren as it drove by our house one day.

Psychic Telepathy or Impressions

This type of communication from Bigfoot to human may be the single most controversial topic in all of Bigfootdom, and splits the ranks like no other subject. I personally believe it happens, because it's happened to my family members and me in one form or another. I have also read about and spoken to others who have had this experience.

For many researchers, though, experience is not proof enough. Wanting "proof" can be a funny thing sometimes, because often there is an attitude that motivates that need. It says, "I need proof so I can understand all the details and take over and control this situation, not to mention how this would benefit me both professionally and financially." I believe it to be true, certainly not just concerning Bigfoot.

Most people do not believe in God because they can't "see" him. Seeing would be their kind of proof. Even if Jesus himself stood in front of people who saw the nail marks on his hands and feet, perhaps even touching him, some would still not believe. Point is, there will ALWAYS be believers and unbelievers, no matter what kind of "proof" is put right of front of them.

Psychic and telepathic communication, or however you want to describe it, is the method of speaking to someone without using audible words, sounds, or signals. It is usually heard in the mind, mind to mind, and many times in distinctive wording that is much more than just an impression, but rather thoughts or pictures.

Some people are rather disturbed about and reject this type of communication because they associate it with a spiritually demonic ability. In their opinion, it should be shunned or avoided. Of course, I agree with this in that regard, but with animals, I am not speaking of the same thing, although it may appear that way.

Bigfoot seems to have a strong ability to communicate with humans by this means. It happened several times with my husband Wayne and our daughter Rachel, as they described while telling their stories.

I, on the other hand, just had strong impressions of their feelings or what they were trying to relate to us. To those of a spiritual world, the Bible calls it "Discerning of Spirits," as described in I Corinthians.

Stick and Rock Formations

Another type of controversial, non-verbal communication between the creatures themselves is known as "stick formations." They are found on the ground or up in trees in various patterns, and are made of sticks or branches. Possible formations may include arches, teepees, Xs, crosses, and stars, just to name a few. Some believe that each one might have a specific meaning, giving information to another Bigfoot. They could be trail markers for migration points, or might translate as "do not enter," directions to a Bigfoot gathering, the size or number of mountains yet to cross, messages like these. However, at this time, most researchers believe the formations to be natural occurrences in nature and not created by a Bigfoot.

Other formations have been found made with various sizes of large stones or rocks. Rocks seem to be piled up in certain structures to perhaps also to send messages of some sort.

Infrasound

This phenomenon is the strangest of all the types of communication under consideration. Infrasound is sound that is so low that the human ear cannot hear it. However, it can have effects on the human body, such as nausea, headaches, extreme fatigue, blurred vision, disorientation, difficulty in moving, dizziness, becoming very emotional, and particularly fear, anxiety, or dread.

There are countless reports of people in a "hot spot" of Bigfoot activity reporting such temporary symptoms. I can personally relate to and testify to these. I remember several evenings experiencing severe fear. As long as it was light outside, I was fine, but when darkness came and I was aware of or heard Bigfoot around the house, it was a different story.

A couple of times, it was so bad that I had to take a gun with me into the office building that was literally only three feet from the house. I took a dog with me inside, turned up the music, and locked the door behind me! I knew I was quite safe and I really was not afraid of seeing a Bigfoot, but this fear thing was all over me like a blanket. Remember, I knew nothing at all at the time about infrasound.

Other animals such as lions, tigers, or elephants use infrasound to freeze their prey before attacking. It may also be used as a warning device to scare away their enemies. In some cases, governments have used infrasound for crowd control.

In the Bigfoot world, an increasing number of people are experiencing some of these strange symptoms. Those to whom it has happened in the past are just beginning to get vocal about it. I've heard of individuals having abdominal and other types of cramping when in an area of Bigfoot presence. Others have even claimed that they cannot move or were frozen for a short period of time. There are even women who have admitted that they began menstruating while out in the woods in a "hot spot" of activity, despite having just finished a normal monthly period. Since it's mostly men who are out in the field, this topic is not openly discussed. Could this be the result of infrasound?

Wayne and I have had the experience of being "scanned," mostly in our minds. Could this, too, be the result of infrasound?

Some researchers have been threatened with loss of status within certain groups if they even speak of these strange happenings.

Ultrasound

This is on the other end of the scale. This is sound that is too high for most human ears to hear. Ultrasound has a sonar-type quality to it; bats use it to send out signals that will bounce off objects and return, relaying information on an object's size, shape, and distance away. This makes moving around in darkness easy.

Dolphins and whales communicate using ultrasound/sonar methods. Ultrasound generator systems are sold with claims that the high pitch frightens away rodents and insects. Very high ultrasound can actually disintegrate certain cells, including bacteria.

A man who had seen a Bigfoot earlier in his life was out deer hunting not so many years ago. While sitting up in a deer stand, he began to hear a low humming that seemed to be coming from all around him, he says. He thought he saw something in the trees, but, being somewhat familiar with the *presence* of a Bigfoot from experiences in previous years, he believed the sound came from a Bigfoot.

Ultrasound can be used to measure the thickness or density of an object. Again, there are countless reports from those out in the field of "feelings" of being scanned or probed. This could possibly explain that sensation.

Static Electrical Charge

This is a newer theory. Is it possible that Bigfoot creatures have some type of static electrical field in or around them?

It is not uncommon for a person to report, the hair on my neck, or arms, or even on my head, stood straight up. And they mean it literally.

What about all the batteries in the cameras, flashlights, night-vision scopes, or voice recorders that were "working just fine" one minute and were completely dead the next. I have even read accounts of electrical car parts dying.

Could this also be the answer to the mystery of why a Bigfoot's eyes seem to be illuminated from inside its own body? In other words, their eyes shine in the dark without any light reflecting off of them.

I believe it is a very real possibility that because of the physical and emotional effects that infrasound, ultrasound, and static electrical charge have on humans, they may be interpreted by some as paranormal activity.

Those researchers who only collect "scientific evidence," interpreting these things as paranormal and ignoring them, may indeed be missing out on some essential information that may answer some very important questions in the long run.

6. THEORIES OF ORIGIN: WHAT IS A BIGFOOT?

What is a Bigfoot and where did they come from? No one knows the answer to those questions for sure, but we have gathered ten theories in the following list, although there are probably more. We believe that Bigfoot are part of creation, have been around a long time, and are indigenous to this earth. Here is our list:

1. North American primate
2. Prehistoric ape: *Gigantopithecus blacki*
3. Prehistoric Neanderthal man: The missing link
4. Forest people, Stick Indians, Sasquatch, Native American "Brothers"
5. Esau, the very hairy brother of Jacob in the Old Testament of the Bible
6. Cain, the firstborn son of Adam and Eve in the Biblical account
7. Giants / Nephelim / Fallen Angels
8. Demonic shape-shifting spirits
9. Multi dimensional beings connected with UFOs
10. A new species

North American Primate

This is probably the most common theory. Bigfoot is simply a two-legged ape that has not yet been scientifically identified, because scientists have not yet examined a living or dead specimen.

Many people today actually believe that every kind of animal, insect, and so on, has been discovered and documented worldwide. This is far from the truth. Even now, hundreds of new species are being discovered and identified every year.

Most people would agree that most species of chimpanzees, apes, and other primates have astonishing intelligence, and I would agree. However, the intelligence that Bigfoot creatures exhibit on a continual basis seems to be far above the capacity of any primate. They stay hidden from their biggest and most dangerous predator, humans, and survive generation after generation. Their ability to communicate with each other and sometimes man is also at a much higher level. Their possible social and family order speaks of something greater than an ape.

Prehistoric Ape

Many believe that Bigfoot is a descendent of a prehistoric and extinct ape called *Gigantopithecus blacki*. Remains of this ape, including many sets of massive jaws and teeth, have been found in China and Vietnam. They estimate this creature to have been 10 or more feet tall and at least 1,200 pounds in weight. According to the late Dr. Grover Krantz, they are found in the fossil record.

Perhaps modern-day Bigfoot is an offshoot of this prehistoric ape, but, then again, it would be categorizing these creatures as a primate, and I believe they may be more than that.

Prehistoric Neanderthal Man: The Missing Link

I suppose by some stretch of the imagination, one could picture a man covered in hair with a thick, protruding brow, a large flat nose, a large mouth with long thin lips, and oversized yellowish teeth. This happened progressively over a period of billions of years, the result of a slimy amoeba crawling its way out of the water onto land and beginning to change its shape and size to become the hairy man mentioned above. But wait! Some stayed that way, while most of the other ones continued to change until they eventually started looking like we do now. Wow! The missing link!

Okay, so I'm a bit sarcastic here. Believing as we do in a personal Creator, this sounds too ridiculous! My uncle Louie wasn't an ape-man. We were made in the image of God Himself. Sorry, I can't even imagine this.

Forest People, Stick Indians, Native American "Brothers"

"Sasquatch" is a name that came from a Canadian Indian tribe. Native American legends of what or who Sasquatch is obviously vary from tribe to tribe. There is, however, a considerable majority who believe that Sasquatch are human, not ape or animal, part of a wild or rogue Indian tribe that lives in the forests and possesses supernatural powers. Therefore, they are "brothers" and should be protected and respected. I have also heard of others who say that the Stick Indians are really evil spirits. One man claims he was almost thrown over a cliff by some of them and had to strongly resist them.

As we have continued to learn about Bigfoot this past year since leaving the coast of Washington and to hear of others' experiences, our opinion on what a Bigfoot really is has changed. We used to believe that they were some sort of uncategorized species of animal, but because of our own personal experience and what we have learned from others, I think it's safe to say at this point that we now believe them to be more human than animal. We now call them Forest People.

Esau, the Hairy Brother of Jacob in the Old Testament

This theory of Bigfoot is based on the Bible, Genesis 25:20.

In Genesis 25:20 begins the story of Isaac marrying Rebekah. She was barren, Isaac sought the Lord, and she conceived.

22: And the children struggled together within her and she said, (paraphrasing)

"What is going on in there, Lord?"

23: And the Lord said unto her, "Two nations are in your womb, and two manner of people shall be separated from you; and the one people shall be stronger than the other people; and the elder shall serve the younger."

24: There were twins in her womb.

25: And the first came out red, all over like a hairy garment; and they called his name Esau.

29: Esau was a cunning hunter, and a man of the field.

Esau was the first in line to receive the family's inheritance and blessings upon the death of his father Isaac. He despised his birthright and sold it to Jacob, his brother, one day for a bowl of lentils that Jacob had made.

Chapter 27:1: And it came to pass that when Isaac was old, and his eyes were dim, so that he could not see, he called Esau, his eldest son and said unto him, "My son," and Esau said, "Here I am."

2-6: And Isaac said, "Behold, now I am old and I do not know the day of my death. Now, therefore, take your weapons, your quiver and bow, go out to the field, and get me some venison. And make me some savory meat like I love, and bring it to me so I may eat, and that my soul may bless you before I die." Rebekah heard Isaac speaking to Esau. And Esau went to the field to hunt for venison. Rebekah told Jacob what she had overheard and sent Jacob out to kill two kid goats and to bring the meat so he could give it to his father, and receive a blessing from his father before he died.

11-13: And Jacob said to Rebekah, "Esau my brother is a hairy man, and I am a smooth man. My father will feel, and he shall know that I am deceiving him. I shall bring a curse and not a blessing upon myself." His mother said, "May the curse be upon me. Just go do what I said."

14: Jacob brought the meat to his mother.

15: And Rebekah took some clothing of Esau's and had Jacob put them on. And she put the skins from the goat kids upon Jacob's hands and upon the smooth of his neck.

17-18: She gave the meat and bread to Jacob, and he took them unto Isaac. His father said, "Who are you, my son?"

19: Jacob said, "I am Esau, your first born. I have done like you asked. Sit up and eat of my venison, so your soul may bless me".

20: And Isaac said, "How did you get this venison so quickly?" Jacob answered, "Because the Lord your God brought it to me."

21: And Isaac said. "Come over here so that I may feel you to see if you are Esau or not."

22: And Jacob went over to Isaac and he felt him. Isaac said, "The voice is Jacob, but the hands are the hands of Esau."

23: And Isaac didn't realize it was really Jacob because his hand was hairy like Esau's hand, so he blessed Jacob.

The Bible goes on to say that as Isaac blessed Jacob, he smelled his clothes, which smelled like the fields. When Esau came in later and found out what had happened, he was bitterly upset and planned to kill Jacob, but Rebekah his mother sent Jacob to live with her brother.

I decided to include such details in this story, because this theory stirs up some interesting questions. Why was a newborn baby so hairy? The reddish color, I can understand.

Was there a DNA malfunction? There is a rare genetic mutation that causes hypertrichosis, which is abnormal hair growth all over the body. This disease is so rare that today there are only around 100 people in the entire world who suffer from the problem. They are sometimes called

"Wolf-men" (and women, too). Other forms of hypertrichosis are not as rare, but this genetic abnormality is the only one that produces normal hair covering the entire body.

There are three reasons for this theory of Bigfoot coming from Esau: 1) The extreme hairiness all over his body; 2) The Lord telling Rebekah while the twins were in her womb that she was carrying "two nations" and "two manner of people"; and 3) Esau was a "cunning hunter and a man of the field." An interesting story. Rather strange for an infant to be THAT hairy and grow up to be a hairy man. I can accept a man that hairy if he had a genetic problem, but a newborn? As an adult, he married a Canaanite woman, which terribly grieved the hearts of his parents because, again, the Canaanites were considered a cursed and ungodly people. His lineage became known as the Edomites (Edom means "red.")

If you look at a close-up of Michelangelo's famous painting, *The Last Judgment*, some say that the Edomites are huddled together near a large rock and, if you look closely, you can see that they resemble today's version of Bigfoot.

Cain and Other Biblical Interpretations

The Journal of Mormon History suggests that Sasquatch is really Cain, the jealous and murderous first son of Adam and Eve in the Bible.

Genesis 4:8: And Cain talked with Abel his brother, and it came to pass when they were in the field that Cain rose up against Abel his brother, and slew him.

9: And the Lord said unto Cain, "Where is Abel your brother?" And he said, "I don't know, am I my brother's keeper?"

10: And the Lord said, "What have you done? The voice of your brother's blood cries up to me from the ground [grave].

11: "And now you are cursed from the earth, which has opened her mouth to receive your brother's blood from your hand.

12: "When you till the ground, it shall not yield unto you her strength; a fugitive and a vagabond shall you be on the earth."

13: And Cain said unto the Lord, "My punishment is greater than I can bear.

14: "Behold, you have driven me out this day from the face of the earth, and from your face shall I be hid; and I shall be a fugitive and a vagabond on the earth: and it will come to pass that everyone that finds me shall kill me."

15: And the Lord said unto him, "Therefore whoever kills Cain, vengeance shall be taken on him sevenfold." And the Lord set a mark upon Cain, lest any finding him should kill him.

The Bible goes on to give accounts of Cain's wife, children, grandchildren, and several generations after that. To believe that Sasquatch actually came from Cain because he was cursed and declared "a fugitive and a vagabond" is taking scripture too literally.

In that case, if our hands offend us, we should cut them off, and if our eyes offend us, we should pluck them out, as is written in the words of Jesus.

After reading this biblical account of Cain, one can see that there was a type of curse pronounced on him as the first murderer. Some believe that Eve actually had sexual intercourse with the devil, and that Cain and the generations after him until this day are the seed of the devil and irredeemable.

Another interesting account of biblical curses is found in the book of Daniel. Daniel was a Hebrew, a follower of the Law of Moses living in the ungodly land of Babylon, whose king was Nebuchadnezzar at that time. King Nebuchadnezzar was a powerful king and is mentioned repeatedly in at least nine books of the Old Testament. He and his armies conquered city after city, enlarging his own kingdom of Babylon and making it a great empire. The king began having disturbing dreams and called for interpretations from his magicians, astrologers, and sorcerers. Daniel was called upon to first recount the dream and then to interpret it, which according to scripture he did accurately through the wisdom of God's Spirit. The king was so impressed that he wanted everyone to honor Daniel's God, but soon after that he himself did the opposite. He was full of pride and bragged that the Babylonian Empire's greatness was due to his own strength, despite the fact that for years God had spoken through his prophets that He would give many cities over to Nebuchadnezzar… and He did.

Then came the fulfillment of one of the dreams: a curse was laid on the king. In the Book of Daniel 4, the account states that Nebuchadnezzar was "driven away from men, began to eat grass as oxen, his body was wet with the dew of heaven (he lived outside), his hairs were grown like eagle's feathers (dreadlocks?), and his nails were as bird's claws". He remained this way for seven years, again according to his own dream, until he "looked up to heaven to praise and honor God as the TRUE king."

I bring out this particular story because there are those who believe that these Bigfoot creatures are very human and have been cursed in the ancient past. They are waiting for some kind of redemption or deliverance from their present plight.

Giants, Nephilim, Fallen Angels

This is yet another theory of the origin of Bigfoot based on information found in the Bible, a theory that many believe to be credible and even probable.

In Genesis 6:4 it says, "There were giants in the earth in those days; and also after that, when the sons of God came unto the daughters of men, and they bare children to them, the same became mighty men which were of old, men of renown."

Job 1 tells us that Satan was considered a "son" of God. The above verse in Genesis is therefore speaking of fallen (evil) angels. They came unto human women, had sexual intercourse with them, and the women had children who were all violent. These children are considered Nephilim. Nephilim is from the root word "Naphel," which is translated as "fallen ones." Some were giants (larger in body), perhaps like Goliath in the biblical story of David and Goliath. Others were not necessarily large, but were still a mixed breed of spirits and humans. Many believe that Nephilim still are upon the earth today.

The Bible goes on to say,

5: And God saw that the wickedness of man was great in the earth, and that every imagination of the thoughts of his heart was only evil, continually.

6: And it repented the Lord that he made man on the earth, and it grieved him at his heart.

7: And the Lord said "I will destroy man whom I have created from the face of the earth; both men and beast and the creeping things, and the fowls of the air; for it repenteth me that I have made them."

12: God looked upon the earth and it was corrupt: for all flesh had corrupted his way upon the earth.

13: God said to Noah, "The end of all flesh has come before me, for the earth is filled with violence."

Of course, we know what happened then. It rained for forty days and forty nights. Dr. Carl Baugh of the Creation Museum in Glenrose, Texas, and other scientists believe that before the flood, there was a canopy of water up in the earth's atmosphere that created a terrarium-like climate on earth and maintained mild temperatures over the entire globe. It was this canopy that apparently fell apart, coming down to the earth and causing rain for the first time since creation.

I only emphasize this account because these giant offspring must have been terribly violent for God to destroy them and all flesh.

The Bible states in Matthew 24:37 and Luke 21 that "as in the days of Noah," Jesus would return to earth. Are we in those days?

Could alien abductions that we hear so much about today be fallen angels still messing with humans? Some give credence to the Book of Enoch, where there are detailed accounts of fallen angels and giants, besides other stories. However, others say there are too many discrepancies in the text: it couldn't have been written in the stated time period; hence, most scholars disregard such theories.

Tablets from the earliest human civilization known, the Sumerians, contain accounts of the Anunnaki (which some say is another name for the fallen angels) and their relationship with mankind. An offspring, a female, of one of these angels and a woman, claimed to have created a large, strong, hairy beast to stand against her own son, supposedly an overbearing brute and a bully. He was a King named Gilgamesh. The beast lived in the forest with the wildlife and was actually called "forester." There are those who believe that this was the origin of the Bigfoot creatures.

"The concept of giants appears in every country's mythology, from Greek and Roman to the Norsemen and most Native American tribes. Many myths and legends began with a truth. Could Bigfoot be a remnant of the giants of old?" asks Ron Morehead of Sierra Sounds.

For some mind-blowing pictures, histories, and facts on giants then and now, visit the website www.stevequayle.com.

Demonic Shape-Shifting Spirits

There are those who sincerely believe that the Bigfoot are spirits, evil spirits that have the ability to change from one form to another.

Even though "spirits" are thought of by most as ghost-like, invisible beings, they can show themselves in a physical form. Some explain the stories where "they were there right in front of me, and then they simply disappeared" by using the theory that Bigfoot are spirits.

Through certain religious ceremonies, sometimes involving the use of psychedelic drugs or even natural items like mushrooms and common herbs, some believe that one enter into an evil part of the spirit world and learn to shape-shift.

In our own experiences with Bigfoot in our backyard, we never sensed any evil, nor did we ever feel that our lives were threatened in any way. If Bigfoot are shape-shifters, our experience suggests that they are not evil ones.

Multi-Dimensions: UFO Connections

This theory is very popular in some parts of the Bigfoot community. Many, many stories have been documented in which a Bigfoot was sighted along with orbs, large and small colored lights, mechanical noises like motors running or doors opening and closing, even visible UFO spaceships. Some claim to have actually seen Bigfoot entering spaceships or coming and going into portals in the earth.

The phenomenon of the "disappearing" Bigfoot (mentioned in the preceding section) can also be explained by this theory. It is thought that they and/or UFOs also come and go into different dimensions that exist, but cannot be seen by the human eye. We have even heard that some believe that Bigfoot are pets to aliens, and are let out of their spaceships at night.

We never had such activity at our house, but Barb, the woman investigator who came and stayed with us for many nights and lived in the house for six months after we moved, did have several experiences like this, although not at our house. She was out on several nights with other researchers in an area heavy with Sasquatch presence. She and another man saw large orbs, small lights of various colors that came very close to her body and then popped and vanished. They heard a loud motorized noise that sounded like a heavy door closing in the earth, while at the same time they saw a couple of Bigfoot coming down a gravel road who were there one minute and gone the very next.

Another long-term witness says he has seen up to 100 light orbs in a heavily populated Bigfoot area. We agreed that the lights may be the result of electromagnetic static coming from Bigfoot bodies, as I have mentioned earlier. We humans have similar static on our bodies — just rub a balloon on your head — but the Bigfoot may have a great deal more operating on a higher level.

Another thought, let's say that there actually are UFOs or aliens from other stars. What if they have some kind of ability to manipulate, control, and use these Bigfoot creatures for their own purposes? The forest people would have to be constantly on the lookout for the aliens above and humans on the earth. The stress of bare survival would be unreal!

If you ever go on a night walk with no flashlights or any light of any sort in an area where there are Bigfoot, you might have strange experiences of your own.

A New Species

Last, but only on this particular list, is the belief that Bigfoot is a brand new, yet undocumented, or unknown species. Bigfoot DNA has been determined by researchers to be approximately 95% human and 5% chimpanzee. The latter's DNA is also close to human. However, that "conclusion" was based on DNA that was then available to that group of scientists; it was never incontrovertibly proven to be Bigfoot DNA.

Through our brief experiences and the feelings we received from these beings, it is now impossible for us to call them "animals," considering their human-like behaviour and appearance. Soon, and we believe we are on the verge of major discoveries, Bigfoot will be classified in a new way. There are already two counties in the state of Washington that consider killing a Bigfoot murder.

7. Epilogue

We hope you enjoyed this simple but true account of our encounters with Bigfoot creatures during the six months we lived on the west coast of Washington State. Perhaps you have learned something about these creatures through our research and other stories we've included. What is your theory? Where did they come from and what are they *really,* ape or human? Please feel free to contact us with your feedback at our website, www.bigfootbook.net or email us at forestpeoplevisits@yahoo.com.

During the writing of this book, we were encouraged to think back to other incidents in our lives that could have been Bigfoot related. In Wayne's story, he told you about a large rock being thrown back at him after he'd thrown it behind him. He also recalled the night he saw a dark figure running through the small valley near our house and the wood knocks he'd heard. Remember, at that time we had no clue at all about Bigfoot behavior. We were under the impression that it was men training for government security reasons.

When we moved to Washington, looking back now, we had some experiences that could also have been Bigfoot activity, but we didn't know it at the time. We lived on a 1,200-acre ranch in a rural area with a wilderness of thick forest around us. Behind and to the south of our house was a small, narrow valley with a creek running through it. To the north were hundreds of acres of hayfields where each night sometimes up to 80 deer would graze. We saw a few bears over a period of three years, but not many. Coyotes were plentiful and very bold, and they would sometimes come very near the house looking for food, our young granddaughter, or several litters of puppies, a tasty treat for them. Coyotes were in abundance and would yelp and bark like they were half insane.

My husband Wayne would adamantly declare that "something or someone" was watching us from behind the house. Our daughter Rachel "felt" it also, and would spend time with her binoculars scanning the hills to see if she could see anything. I used to tease my husband that maybe video cameras had been placed up in the trees just to spy on us. However, there were several times I had the eerie feeling of being watched, or I would hear noises outside the office window where I spent a lot of time managing our home business, but that was only at night.

Since my hubby is a late night person, he has experienced the most encounters. Again, one evening while outside looking at the stars, he had a strong feeling of someone looking at him from near the chicken coop and barn, about sixty yards behind and north of the house, a very dark area on that moonless night.

One evening, I was sitting in the living room, when suddenly I heard very loud vibrating footsteps as something ran past the front door. One of our dogs was in the room with me, and she sat up and growled. The next morning, I realized that I had left the gate by the swing set open. You see, the immediate yard around the house was fenced in by a white wooden fence that was reinforced by chicken wire to keep "whatever" out. There was a gate on the hay field side near the swing set and one in back facing the chicken coop and barn. And the driveway to the house had a cattle guard at the end where the fencing stopped.

Anyway, I was questioning what could have been big enough to make such loud noises. A horse perhaps, but there were no loose horses around. I thought perhaps an elk, another large animal, so I went looking for elk prints. I found nothing. Bigfoot never entered my mind because I really didn't know anything about them, although I believed in them. Whatever it was had to be very heavy and quick.

A couple of months before we moved to the coast, I was driving home from town down a winding two-lane mountain road alongside the Columbia River. As I came to a wooded area on my left, I saw a cloudy white, transparent Bigfoot shape in front of me walking (so it seemed) slightly above the ground toward the road. Then it totally disappeared. Now, I am not one who sees things out of the ordinary, although I do believe in a spirit world. It did not frighten or distract me.

I recently shared this incident on a radio talk show, strange as it is, and the co-host responded that something very similar had happened to her many years ago. She had never shared her story with anyone until that evening on the radio because she thought no one would believe her.

When I shared this incident recently with some people at a Bigfoot forum, they suggested that it was actually a Bigfoot, and that they seem to have the ability to "cloak" themselves, hence the disappearing act. I don't know if I believe that. Maybe it was a vision of things yet to come, who knows.

Wayne and I seriously debated whether or not to add the following information, knowing that it might be misunderstood or deemed impossible, since it would involve having Bigfoot activity at several places we had lived. Truth is, it is not unusual that a person may have an ongoing series of experiences over a period of years or even a lifetime. I'll let Wayne tell you in his own words the events that have taken place since we've been in Oregon.

Moving from Washington to Oregon, our encounters with the Bigfoot folk continued for over a year. We knew from earlier reports that Sasquatch had been seen in the forests and mountains of Oregon where we were relocating, so we were always on the lookout, as we'd been while living on the Pacific Northwest coast. Approximately three months after relocating to another residence in Oregon, to our big surprise, we began to have more encounters with Sasquatch.

It began when I went out into the wilderness about 22 miles by road from the new house, but only about 12 miles if one could go straight across the valley. I had been traveling up a gravel road off of a small main road, going deeper into the forest, when I stopped to get out and check out the area. What I'm about to relate may sound almost unreal, but when I walked six steps past the front of the car, I looked down to my right and there was a Bigfoot footprint in the ground going up a small incline just a few feet off the road. My first thought, beyond recognizing the print, was that I had just driven up to and walked right up to a

Bigfoot print — a total and curious coincidence. Like, I'm not even looking for them, same as over on the coast, and here we go again.

The footprint wasn't as big as the ones we'd seen in our yard and on

Figure 14: Track in Oregon.

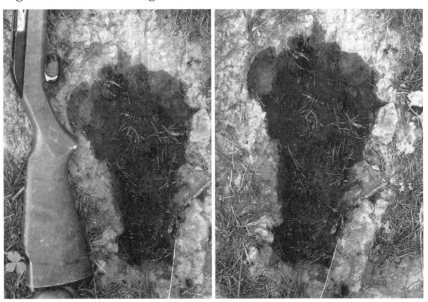

Figure 15: Close-up of the track.

the surrounding land over on the Pacific Northwest coast, but it still measured about 14" long with the very wide spread at the front, much wider than normal human feet. I didn't have a tape measure with me at the time, so I used my rifle to strike a measure on it for later reference with a tape measure, and I also lined up my boot-covered foot next to it. I then took pictures of the footprint with comparisons to my boot and to the rifle. It was only one footprint sunk at least one inch into the ground, and it was directed straight into the bushes and trees lining the road and beyond.

I checked for more prints and trail marks in the immediate area, but I saw nothing. The ground lying in the direction the footprint was headed was covered in short groundcover and brush, so it wasn't a good place for making footprints.

About this footprint and some others I am about to mention, I want to emphasize that they were on land that is very rough, due to an abundance of rocks, big and small. The soil there is interspersed with small rocks, many of them sharp-edged, and it is nothing like walking on dark topsoil, which makes easy indentations. So if someone is wondering if the footprints we saw could be human, I will assure you that this rocky ground would shred a human's feet quickly, and that would be the end of that. And as a reminder, this first print that I saw was at least an inch deep in this rough, rocky terrain, indicating to me that it was made by someone with a body of great weight compared to even big humans. I walked on this ground making no prints, and I weigh about 170 pounds.

Now after I had finished photographing this footprint, I hid it, covering it with nearby dry tree limbs to make that spot look like any other around there, just another place where old dried limbs had fallen in the past. I did this with the intention of bringing Julie out there later to show her, which I did very soon afterwards. When she and I went back out there to the footprint site and after she'd seen it, we started walking around the area looking for more footprints and other evidence of Bigfoot's presence. Sure enough, about 700 yards away from that footprint, I saw some juvenile Bigfoot prints about 50 yards off the road. These were only about eight inches long, and were made in the same kind of rough soil. Inspired by these other finds, we decided to go back to the small main paved road that had brought us out to the back roads we were on, so that we could go further into the wild.

Traveling about three miles deeper into the wilderness, we eventually decided on a spot to stop. We had to walk over and past many fallen trees that were on the way up a draw. This led to a clearing of tall grasses below a line of forest that went on up a big mountain. Now we were about a quarter mile from the road with a big view of the surrounding area. To our surprise, we ran across more juvenile Bigfoot prints similar to the size of the smaller ones we had just seen a few miles back. So now I began to think, are we actually going directly where the Sasquatch go, or are there that many in the area that we can scarcely miss seeing evidence of them regardless of where we go. This was the same rough ground as where we had just come from. I took photos of these footprints, but the pictures didn't turn out as good as I would have liked. I even poured water into the prints hoping that would help, but it only helped a little, and not really enough. So, these footprints were the first sign that we again lived in Bigfoot territory.

Approximately six months after we had arrived in Oregon, we started having Sasquatch experiences at our house. The house actually had a large mountain range as its backyard. One very rugged mountain started in our backyard and went right up about 5,000 feet, with evergreen forest, massive rock formations, and also caves along the way up.

Now, concerning Bigfoot experiences at our house in Oregon, here I go. Early on a very windy night, I decided to pick up Julie's Irish whistle and go out onto the front deck to the end farthest from the front door, where I could easily view the forest behind the house and look upward through the many 80-foot-tall trees, searching for the tall ones who live among them.

On the whistle I was mostly expressing improvised sounds rather than melodies. I preferred using the whistle outside rather than inside, but I was also using it outside hoping there were Sasquatch among those trees, and that they could "hear" me (meaning that I was one who knew they exist, and I was one who was not out to "get 'em").

I was sounding that whistle without yet knowing how well the sound was traveling up the mountain. Days later, when I went up there, I happened to hear Sophie the border collie barking down at the house on that same deck. I realized that her bark traveled up the mountain fast, loud, and clear. It sounded like she was only 20 yards away, when in fact I might have been 500 yards from home near some caves. So I realized then that, sure enough, on the night I had sent out the sounds of the Irish whistle, the sound would have gone far up the mountain, where it could be heard by anyone who was up there to hear it.

Actually, the Irish whistle information will help to clarify what's next. At around 2:30 AM, much later on the same night when I had improvised on the whistle in the strong winds that were being vortexed through the mountain canyons where we lived, I had a visitor come near the house. This happened as I had just walked into one of the rooms at the front of the house and turned on a light. Immediately as I turned on the light, and I mean *instantly*, this early-morning visitor sounded back to me. What sounded like a male Sasquatch answered my Irish whistle signals with such quickness in relation to my turning on the light that it was as though he had previous knowledge of our behavior, like regularly turning on our lights in the early morn.

He sounded like he was right down the driveway about 25 yards from the house. He made two distinct howls, one right after the other.

Figure 16: Caves near the house in Oregon.

When I heard the howls, it seemed as though he was responding directly to the Irish whistle sounds.

These howls he made contrasted with my "happy and fun" sounds on the whistle. My interpretation of these sounds is that they were made in a state of distress or concern. I don't think it was about food, because there was always an abundance of deer in the area. It was like he deliberately wanted to get that message or something similar across to me. I've heard some of their happy sounds and what I call their regular howls, similar to the howling that we have on our website, but this was different. This incident would be a first encounter at the Oregon house with our Bigfoot neighbors.

The next encounter I had was among those caves far up behind our house. In the past, I had hiked up the mountain beyond the caves long before I knew there was anyone living there. Since that Bigfoot visitor had come to our house howling at me, I figured they must not be too far from us, being close enough to hear the Irish whistle sounds that night. So, I went up the mountain for a look-see, hoping to find some kind of clue as to where they might be.

When I got to within approximately one hundred yards of the caves nearest our house and started examining them, I was confronted with a strong warning feeling in my gut area telling me, "Stop where you are and come no closer." I looked all around in the rocks, bushes, trees, and up the trees to see if it might be a cougar, but saw nothing. I have smelled cougar when they were close by or had recently been in an area, but there was nothing like that. And, I wasn't really looking for bears, because in my experience, they are pretty easy to spot and they usually run from me as soon as they see me with no ill feelings directed towards me. Also from my past experience, where Bigfoot are, bears are scarce. I went back to the house a few minutes later, beginning to be convinced that I might have discovered approximately where the forest people lived.

A week or so later, going up the mountain and coming into clear sight of the caves, there was suddenly a mimic woodpecker sound among the trees surrounding those caves. I say mimic because I have heard, watched, and filmed woodpeckers through the years, and they have never sounded like what I heard. It seemed obvious to me that the woodpecker sound was in response to my approaching their dwelling, like one of them signaling others. (Shortly, I will explain how I know there were others.)

This woodpecker sound wasn't the result of pecking wood at all. It was way too consistent in sound and rhythm to be an actual woodpecker looking for bugs in a tree. It's easy to distinguish whether a woodpecker sound is coming from wood being pecked, or if it is a sound made directly into the air, like chipmunks or squirrels would do. I estimate that the pecking sound was ten times louder than any woodpecker I have ever heard, including the fairly big ones I've seen. The eight to ten extremely loud pecking sounds that were made all sounded almost exactly alike. This is also inconsistent with how woodpeckers peck as they look for bugs hidden in the trees. Woodpeckers seek out bugs in the trees using their beaks at various angles and with varying amounts of force.

During the many times I have watched woodpeckers, they saw me nearby and just continued with their bug search, pecking away at the trees. When this loud pecking sound happened, though, I never saw any birds, nor did I hear any other woodpecker sounds. So, I just continued up the mountain and on beyond what I now believed was their dwelling place in the caves.

Within a week of the woodpecker sound incident, I went up beyond those caves two times after believing that I had discovered where they lived. Their caves just happened to be right next to one of the easier routes up the mountain starting from behind our house. So as a result, there are some paths that have been worn there near these caves. These paths actually go up to the side and right across the top of them.

The second time I went up past the caves, I noticed an obvious sign of their presence: there were five or six big trees pushed down across the path that went right above the caves, right where I walked. Julie and I have read and heard that this kind of behavior is typical; that is, they block paths around their territory, seeking to discourage visitors from getting close to them. Considering this, it helps to figure in the fact that I was probably the only person traveling up those paths in the short period of time between my first and second hike through there, because there were hardly any other people in that area during that time.

As a side note, when I was standing on the part of the path that goes right along the top of their caves, looking out I saw that they had a great view from their "front door" of mountains and the surrounding area. I also realized that back on the Pacific Northwest coast, the Bigfoot shelter I'd found was also in a place where they could step outside their shelter and instantly have a great view of the Olympic Mountains. Do these two examples indicate their appreciation of nature's beauty?

Later, I had more visitations from the forest people. As I made some tunes on a guitar late at night, I received telepathic images from them. It was very similar to what had happened at the house on the coast when I played the guitar at night. I estimate that because I was using an electric guitar with headphones, although the guitar can still be heard a little, the Bigfoot must have been fairly close to our house to hear the music. Similar to the experience at the other house, when I was not thinking about Bigfoot at all, the image of a brown-haired male Bigfoot from the neck up, with much hair on the face, appeared vividly in my mind. He was not looking directly at me, but almost at a forty-five degree angle to me, and the image in my head was about two inches high by one inch wide.

The second time a telepathic message was sent to me while making notes on the guitar, it turned out to be a different brown-haired male Bigfoot. This one didn't have any hair on his face though, and his face looked very similar to some humans I have seen before. Doesn't that raise some interesting questions? Both times I was not thinking about them at all, and both times their images appeared in my mind about the same size in very vivid color and detail, clearer than a lot of my own imaginings.

Appearing in my mind on two different nights, neither of the facial images of the male Bigfoot was looking directly at me, like the male image back on the coast. Both of their faces were close to that forty-five-degree angle. Considering why their faces were directed at this angle, I realized that I was able to get a good look at them without the imposition of them being "in my face," per se. And similar to the male Bigfoot on the coast, they seemed also to be interested in the music I was enjoying. I could speculate further about why they sent their images into my mind, and also why two of them did this, but I will rest content with simply reporting what I have experienced.

On another late night, Julie was already asleep and I was in the living room. Suddenly (many "suddenlies" with these folks) there was a big bump against the outside wall of our bedroom and the office, which is the next room over on the same outside wall. There was no wind that night, and I checked outside the next morning. There was nothing near that wall that would have made noises like a tree branch falling against the house or rocks thrown. When Julie got up the next morning, she reported having Bigfoot dreams, and then I proceeded to tell her about the bumps in the night.

I also had a couple of experiences late at night while in our bedroom. Julie was already asleep, and I had been lying in bed for about five minutes. Since our bedroom was in the back of the house next to the wilderness that goes right up the mountain, we were somewhat exposed to whatever might walk past our house at night.

That night as I lay awake in bed, someone came running past our window laughing. The laugh sounded mostly like a chimp laugh ("*hee* hee *hee* hee") with some human intonations in it. The attitude of the laugh was like a young prankster just having some late night fun. Wouldn't be surprised if this was the same one who bumped up against the house sometime earlier.

The second experience in the bedroom was one I admit that I didn't like *at all*, and if it happens again I will immediately protest. Before I relate this very unusual occurrence, I need to explain that shortly before this visitation I had recently gone up the mountain near their caves twice, leaving them a banana both times at a place where I believed they could see me. While there, I also talked to them in English, letting them know what I was doing. After my second time leaving a banana, later in the late night, I had just gotten into my place in the bed, lying closest to the back window facing the wilderness. Julie was already asleep. Right after I lay down, I found myself being scanned by one of them. I was scanned by what seemed to me to be one of the adult male Bigfoot.

Strange as it seems, the scan worked in me, going back and forth horizontally a couple of times in my head and then my chest and stomach area. Not only could I feel it happening, but as my eyes were closed, I could see a vertical line on the sides of the scan inside as it went from one side to the other of my head, chest, and stomach. A friend told me that since they can use telepathy, they have the ability to manipulate energy to a degree, making the scan appear to be almost mechanical in nature, like regular lines and a rectangular box. That made sense to me, so I now have a broader understanding of their telepathic abilities. This scanning process happened within about ten seconds. As far as I can tell, it was harmless, though I still felt trespassed against.

As a personal joke I realized that this only happened after the second time I left a banana: maybe since I'd left a chocolate mint patty along with the banana that time, I wondered whether he was looking to see if I had any more of those special treats.

When morning came around, I told Julie of the scanning experience, which I knew she would understand because of what she had learned in her personal research. Well, she informed me that she had awakened apparently not long after I had gone asleep, which I know was soon after I had been scanned. She proceeded to tell me that she, too, had been scanned. She also said that it seemed to be mechanical in nature, and that she could see those lines on the outside of the scanning in her mind as it moved back and forth, also in other directions in her mind a little different from what I'd experienced. We both agreed, though, that the scans were most likely telepathic in nature, rather than mechanical.

After we had lived at the Oregon house for eleven months, I saw one of our forest neighbors. During the daytime I was outside putting together a little igloo-type house for Lilee, our granddaughter, who was now five years old. I built the igloo in clear sight of the forest behind our house, and during that time I began to feel that I was being watched by someone up there in the forest. So I just kept working, but picked a moment to glance quickly into the trees up there. When I did, I saw those characteristic light amber eyes at the side of a big tree located down the mountain in line with their caves. Of course, as soon as I saw them, they instantly moved back behind the tree. It happened quickly, but I appreciate the opportunity to see them.

I want to note that just like the times I'd seen Bigfoot at our house on the coast, there was always a surreal or supernatural feel when I saw them. Every time. I don't know if this is because it's a very unusual, subjective experience, or if it is because it's really a paranormal event.

My last encounter with the forest people in that area happened just a week or so ago, as I finish writing this section. Late at night, I stepped out the front door just to observe in the clear sky the stars and more of what is out there in the universe. Over in the darkness with a little light in the distance, I saw a Sasquatch a hundred yards away from me running across the fields. He or she began running as soon as I stepped outside and looked in their direction. As soon as they had made it across a small field of grass, they hid behind the cover of trees. I then began to have one of those negative feelings up against my gut. As long as I stayed outside looking in their direction, that negative feeling remained in my gut area. Then, as soon as I went back inside the house, the negative feelings instantly stopped. It wasn't exactly like the negative feeling that had hit me up at the caves the first time I examined that spot, but it was similar in that the feelings remained as long as I kept looking in that direction.

I have felt them outside our house several other times, especially when I am in the kitchen fixing something to eat, but only that time did I view them out doing whatever they were doing.

So, that's it for now. This ends my most recent experiences with the Bigfoot folks of the forest. So in finishing up, allow me to state that I believe Bigfoot does exist here on the earth, for I have lived among them.

So that is Wayne's story about our new place.

As I said before, hindsight is so amazing. We questioned ourselves to see if we could have done anything differently. In some things, of course we would have. We wish we could have had many years with them, instead of just six months. We would not have brought all of the researchers with their cameras onto our property. We believe that this would have led to closer contact and a deeper relationship with the forest people. Yes, we believe they are more human than primate — they are wild humans, primitive humans, but humans nevertheless. They seem to have the ability to reason, love, be sad, feel pain, have families, socialize, and so much more. We have learned some things, both good and bad, some things to do and some to avoid. I believe that knowing our ignorance, the Bigfoot tolerated much of our silliness in trying to communicate with them. If you suspect you have such creatures on your property, respect them, feed them (lots), and wait for them to come to you. We are learning, so perhaps they will forgive us, but we've been touched by them and our lives will never be the same again. From this point on, we will always be looking for opportunities to live in areas close to our hairy friends. Meanwhile, the mystery continues....

About the Author

Julie Scott is a wife, the mother of two grown sons and two grown daughters, and the grandmother of two precious granddaughters. She home-schooled her kids for over 20 years, being very active in the home-schooling community. When time allowed, she was a midwife assistant for several years, and is also a trained medical assistant.

Julie is a member of OregonBigfoot and the United Bigfoot Research Group. She is a co-host on a weekly BlogtalkRadio show discussing Bigfoot, the paranormal, and cryptozoology, and has been a guest on several other shows as well. Julie volunteers her time as a contact person for local law enforcement, fish and game, and forest service departments by providing education about Bigfoot sightings in her area. She enjoys gardening, swimming, reading, and walking in the forest.

Julie and her husband, a former contractor, recently sold their world-wide Pinecone/Forest Products business, which they started from scratch and grew to be one of the top five companies of its kind in just seven years. They now reside in northeastern Washington running an internet business, enjoying their grandkids, and "Squatchin" whenever they get the chance.